Fragrant Serenade

Reflections for a Renewed Life

Benny Augustine

FRAGRANT SERENADE

Reflections for a Renewed Life

Benny Augustine

First printing, October 2014

BestRapport Software International Ltd.
53 Cadillac, Kirkland, QC, H9H 4G3
Canada

Paperback ISBN: 978-0-9939155-0-5

Kindle ISBN: 978-0-9939155-1-2

ePub ISBN: 978-0-9939155-2-9

Preface

This book is a collection of poetic reflections that is intended only to inspire and motivate you to lead a renewed life. Each one can derive a different perspective from every poem or reflection that is in this book. I have been jotting down ideas for the past 3 decades whenever I found something interesting and this book is a collection of some of them.

This book contains redemptive writing wherein I swing between the sacred and the secular. You can read from one page to another or randomly select any one of them. The classification of these poems by themes and the index are available at the end of the book.

The ideas and reflections in this book are my own viewpoints and are not in any way related to or affirmed by my employers or organizations - past, present and future.

Let us live our lives by helping others, adjusting our attitudes for the better and singing a Fragrant Serenade to the Divine at all times.

Read, Reflect, Renew…

Enjoy!
Benny Augustine.

Dedication

To my loving parents Augustine and Annakutty

Contents

1. Friendship forever...

I reflect on all the friends who have touched my life.
There are friends who have influenced me and
who have changed my life forever.
I also look back at my friends, who have dropped my friendship or
those with whom I broke up.

There are a few who stood by me every step of the way and
never abandoned me.
Others became my friends only to take advantage of my trust,
money and knowledge.
Some others ganged up together to isolate me,
put me down and to frustrate me.
A few came to me with words of consolation even when
I fell under the weight of the pressures of life.
Some laughed at me when I lost my job, lost my status or
lost something very dear to me.

But you stood by me even when many others abandoned
my friendship and love.
You were there like a true friend protecting me from all harm.
Our love will last forever.
To you I renew my love and friendship.

Our love is immortal and eternal,
Nothing can extinguish the fire of our love.
Nothing can separate us from the love we have for each other,
You are my beloved friend and let no one take away this gem of
friendship.

2. Problem and Opportunity

In every problem, there is an opportunity,
provided I am willing to look for it.
Let me find that opportunity in every problem.

My current situation appears to be a problem, a problem beyond my control.

But I can make the best of these moments to turn them into golden moments, to be cherished in my treasure trove.

Many things that are thrown at me during my life is not by choice and not by chance. Let me transform them and make them acceptable and redeemable in Thy sight.

I will find an opportunity in every problem.

I will see the rainbow even when the clouds are forming above the bright sky.

I will tune my attitude to see things in a positive and enlightened way.

My day and all my tasks would be transformed today…

My problems will melt like snow in the golden rays of
my positive disposition.

When I face a crisis, I don't want to fall into its depths but instead let a cry rise from my heart.

O Master, hear my cry and let my crisis be transformed into an opportunity which only you can perceive at this moment.

You see the present crisis or problem with all its future potential.

Give me the wisdom not to despair even in the
midst of this biggest difficulty.

Give me the courage and strength to bear my daily difficulties and sorrows… let them be turned into wonderful garlands for Thee and into a fragrant offering acceptable in Thy sight.

3. Use objects, Love people

So often have I heard this saying and today I reflect on this for a while.

So many persons just use people and love objects,

just the opposite of what is expected from them.

Many attack people in various ways and consider them problems…

But let me attack problems and respect people.

I have been blaming people wherever I could,

to reduce my responsibility.

But when I blamed others, I have ended up blaming myself.

Help me always to love people and use objects.

I have been constantly blaming my spouse, children, neighbours, students, friends, colleagues, managers, superiors but no one has changed.

Even when I criticize, let me point out the positive first and then what needs to be improved.

It is only in a climate of acceptance and empathy that people will change and give heed to the call for change.

The blame game brings in resistance; empathy brings in acceptance and acceptance brings about change.

I resolve to love people so that their lives will be better.

4. The beauty of life

I reflect on the beauty of life.
It's a multi-coloured beauty that mesmerizes my understanding and wonder.
The beautiful lives of people point to a mystery...
the mystery that life is not fully understandable at any point in time.
The moment you feel that you have understood it all,
It just begins to slip away.

Life is a gift that is to be enjoyed every day of our lives...
Life is a journey that starts at birth and continues at death...
Death is just a transition or a change of form, just like water changes into ice when cold, vapour when hot.

The beauty of life is that it is short and sweet,
to those who know the worth of it.
To others it lingers on like infinity waiting for the Coach to call them off from the field.

5. I change… the world changes

I change, you change
You change, we change
We change, the world changes.

The reluctance and resistance to change is not helpful.
It is just a way to hang on to power, position and status quo.
Every change is painful and so I resist new ideas that support change,
But now I realize that change is a recurring event in my life.

I preach and teach about change, but I really don't want to change,
I try hard to strip myself of my addictions but surely it's a difficult task.
I now realize that I need to change first for others to change,
I understand that I have to take the first step for everyone else to rally for change…
So let me change myself before I set out to change others.

As I sit in meditation at Thy feet, I pledge to be an agent of change
I would act as a catalyst to speed up change.
Change is the only sure and permanent thing.
Permanence is nothing but a string of changes tied together into an Unknown whole.
I marvel at Thy wonders…

The change in seasons which keep on recurring with precision is a wonder,
The change that takes place within me is yet another marvellous wonder.
The attitude to change is a wonderful disposition.
Let me embrace change even if that causes pain.
For it is in this change that my "self" is transformed,
It is in this change that a pupa becomes a butterfly,
It is in this change that a convict becomes a saint.

An attitudinal transformation is all I want.
Let that new disposition keep me open to change like Mother Nature's disposition to help plants
  to sprout in spring,
  grow in summer,
  shed leaves in autumn,
  shiver in winter adorned with ice and snow jewels.
Through all these four seasons, the cycle of change keeps rotating…
Let me change myself so that the world changes...
I have decided to transform myself for the better so that the world changes for the better.

6. Ego and the selfless Self

We have heard it so often - It's when you give that you receive.

Often I find it easy and necessary to amass things for myself,

Rarely do I give things away.

But true joy comes to me only when I give.

St. Francis of Assisi in his prayer mentioned, "It's in giving that you receive".

It is a true and paradoxical statement for endless reflection.

The Greed and all his cousins tempt me to build a castle around my ego and self.

The need is to give and help my brothers and sisters so that we can all dwell in harmony.

The problem with any argument or quarrel is my ego. It is this glorified self that does not want me to see the truth.

My ego wants to be the winner at all times and makes me feel belittled when I give it up.

Let me understand deep in my being that my ego will have to diminish for the selfless self to arise.

The moon and the stars appear when the sun disappears from the sky.

Arise, shine and glow O Divine within me.

Let Thy radiance spread through my body and my entire being.

Let me strip myself of my pride and ego so that my selfless self can work wonders.

This is my prayer unto Thee.

7. Deal or No Need?

Many times, I bought things just because there was a deal.

I am becoming a material person surrounded by a materialistic society,

I become addicted to deals being constantly promoted by the social media.

The ads pop up everywhere I look.

These ads add up to my information overload.

The flyers with the newspapers, the posters on the walls, the e-mails from my web mail, the slow mail from the postal services…

All these vie with each other to grab my attention to make me buy a product or service.

They are clearly placed, cleverly marketed and
tactfully presented to get my attention.

The deals are deals only when I have a need and when that need is fulfilled with various choices…

I have been running after deals that offer rebates and deep discounts.

All these drive me to amass more…

Help me to acquire only that which I really need and not procure things that I won't really use.

Help me to ask myself, "Deal or no Need?" and not "Deal or no Deal?"

Let me pledge to use things and love people,

Reduce my dependence on material goods,

Reuse things whenever and wherever possible,

Recycle stuff that can be recycled.

Let me internalize the maxim: Reduce, Reuse, Recycle.

8. I will ever dream

I will ever dream,

I will never scream even when things go wrong.

I want to contribute to the growth of everyone around me, the society and the whole world.

In a globalized world, the world is one.

We are in it together. We can win together as we are a big family.

I will ever dream of the day when all can have sufficient to live,

I long for the day when all can live peacefully without fear for their safety.

I envision a better world for everyone where all are busy helping to improve our march towards human enlightenment.

I will dream of the day when we will all live happily ever after without hunger, wars and strikes.

It may appear a mythical dream but it is possible and doable.

Let the magic of our dreams come true one day.

Let my dreams be wrapped in reality and I lay them at Thy feet.

O Master, let my dreams be turned into Reality one day.

9. Carpe Diem

I want to pluck the day...

I want to achieve the very best out of this day.

Like a flower, let this day blossom and give forth joy expecting nothing in return.

Let me concentrate today on doing my very best.

Let me make everyone happy who comes into contact with me throughout this day.

Well begun is half done…

I find it difficult to get the best out of my days…

Time management is like a horror movie…

I feel frightened as the time that flies into eternity cannot be brought back,

Seconds, minutes, hours, days, months, years pass by so fast…

Seasons come and seasons go…

Treasons come and treasons go…

Reasons come and reasons go…

I want to live my life to the fullest by making the best use of my time.

I will start this day and enjoy each and every moment …

I will achieve to the best of my ability so that I can partake in the march towards human progress.

Let not trivial distractions turn my attention and concentration away.

Let me give my very best and accomplish great things
out of this precious day.

Let this day bring forth all the joys that I can delight in Thy bliss,
Let this day bring forth the courage to bear all the pains and sorrows.
Let this day be a wonderful day,
Let this day be the best day in my life.

10. Real assets and liabilities

What we consider to be liabilities can become our best assets.
True reflection of what is an asset and a liability can reveal this mystery to us.
Some of our liabilities could be the only assets
left with us at some point in our lives.

Our liabilities can be converted into assets through a change process – a kind of metamorphosis.
I meditate on my assets and liabilities – all that I have achieved and lost so far.
I give up any bitterness that I have accumulated.
I surrender the times of poor judgement.
I am sorry for the times that I hurt others and the environment.
I am deeply repentant of the sins that have reduced my worth.

The greatest gift that I have is the power to change;
The power to change my behaviour and my pattern of life is within me.
I bow my head in silent meditation and take a deep resolve.
I reflect on my present situation and decide to be a new person with renewed enthusiasm and vigour.
I will be a transformed person today.
My liabilities would soon be changed into real assets.
Every day I become a better person and this journey will continue…

11. Call the spade a spade…

Let me reflect on the times that I have been a coward to face the reality and afraid to speak and stand up for truth.

I sugar-coated my words so that it hid the real meaning and focused on some unimportant point.

When change is required, I should not be hesitant to speak up.

I will gather courage to stand up for change.

I have heard of the maxim: "Call the spade a spade".

If I have to call the spade a spade, I should do it.

Let me do that without hurting others.

Often I feel the weight of structures and those in position making unfair decisions and I have no power vested in me to intervene or contribute.

Some of them isolate others to reduce their significance.

The sidelining and even setup for failure happens in every walk of life.

People with similar agenda can flock together
just like birds of the same feather…

They sideline those who are perceived to be against their agenda.

In this world of discrimination and partiality, I should not waver.

Let me do my best to be a good person trying to spread love and peace.

12. Life under the bridge

I was walking under the bridge when I encountered two little children,
Wearing just torn trousers with a piece of bread in their hands.
Their eyes were sunken and there were tears that I could see…
The ribs were all protruding with no flesh,
surely a sign of poverty and malnutrition …

I reached out for a few coins to help them.
They smiled and ran away with a cheer on their faces and a tear in their eyes.
I stopped for a moment and considered their lives and mine.
Why is this difference? Are some born to be poor?
What did they do to deserve such a poor existence?
What can I do to alleviate their misery?

When will a more humane approach begin to take shape?
When will we value every human life just as equal and glorious?
It is for this that I dream and pray that these children will have better days in their lives.

Let me dedicate a part of my resources for their betterment.
Truly, it is in giving that I receive.
I can really find my fulfillment when I give.

13. The Big Picture

So often I hear the words "The Big Picture ".
These days, it is part of the business jargon and corporate lingo...
I reflect on the time on earth as a small fraction of Eternity,
Where the time is limitless, boundless, and timeless.
That is the bigger picture...
I resisted the pains and cried like the new born baby,
Not knowing Thy designs,
How wonderful are Thy deeds,
Let me humbly heed Thy call.
The bigger picture now emerges against the backdrop of eternity.

When my life is lived in the background of eternity,
I will always know my priorities, duties and rights.
I will always act properly keeping in mind this landscape and background.

My life is like a one-act play with no scope for rehearsals,
The curtain can close at any time when the director chooses.
All that matters at the end is not whether I was a hero or how many additional zeroes
I had in my bank account,
It all boils down to how I lived my life.
That's the BIG picture.
There is some time still left for me...let me utilize it to achieve BIG against this background.

14. Every Mountain has a Valley

Just as there is a valley for every mountain,
There are good and bad people everywhere.
It is not good to generalize.
My mind often finds it easier to stereotype people into my myopic vision.

My head finds it easier to group people according to their nationality, country of origin, colour, race, religion and language to serve my jingoistic attitudes and bottle them in fallacious generalizations.
My heart finds it easier to understand nepotism, parochialism, regionalism and everything else that promotes secret discriminations and partiality.
I lay all these at Thy feet.
Let me promote a universal outlook where we all live and work as brothers and sisters.

Is good and bad the two sides of the same coin of Reality?
Suffering – joy, pain – pleasure,
war – peace, birth – death,
matter – antimatter, mortality – immortality.
Is it not the synergy of these opposites the melting pot of Reality?

O Divine Master, Thou art the melting pot of Reality!
I have not even scratched the surface of this Great Reality.
I have not grasped the depths of the wonders of this Reality.
I sit in awe and wonder at Thy feet gasping for words…

15. Chastity, Poverty, Obedience

Today I ponder on the virtues of chastity, poverty and obedience.

These are three vows that religious take but these are also to be observed
by every person.

Chastity is not about celibacy or unmarried status. It is being true to our calling to be pure.

Poverty is the detachment from earthly goods even when we own them.

Obedience is the submission to the will of the Divine in all that we do.

These virtues may be manifested in our families or communities.

They bear witness to the eschatological values in many religions.

The folly of the world is wisdom for those who understand it.

It is in dying to our selfish ways that we are born to peaceful and eternal life.

The politics and power struggle can give us temporary influence over other people, but the real strength comes with an acceptance of other people.

O Master, I lay my strengths and weakness at Thy feet.

For the times I have failed in any of these virtues, I ask for forgiveness and allow me to move on with renewed strength and hope.

Mould and strengthen me to be chaste, poor and obedient to Thy will.

16. Life is short and beautiful

Life is too short and so beautiful to be spoiled
with this fleeting thought or deed.
When I see the shortness of life and the length of time
I spend on material things
I wonder whether my priorities are correct.

There is love, joy and peace to be enjoyed all around me
But I crave for the pleasures of life that are fleeting.
Let me understand the fact that my life is short and that I can make it beautiful for myself and for others around me.
It is my choice to enjoy this life.

Accept my life as a fragrant offering acceptable to Thee.
Let all that I do be pleasing in Thy sight.
O Divine Master, grant me the grace not to sully this beautiful life.
You know Everything… I know just something
which is almost close to Nothing.

Help me to enjoy this short and beautiful life in ways
that are pleasing to You.
Let your wonderful creation be manifested in all its glory through me.
Chisel and polish me to become a wonderful person
pleasing in Thy presence.
Let me enjoy this life with all its beauty and glory.

17. L.O.W.E – Love Only Will Endure

Love only will endure – this is for sure.
This is the unfathomable expression and linkage of our Oneness.
Everything else can pass, but this will be the string that will bind us together.
This is the string theory of love.

Love is the magic that binds us all together,
Love is the light at the end of the tunnel that gives us hope,
Love is the panacea that heals all wounds of strife,
Love is the reason for our living.

True love will endure all strife and struggles,
It longs for peace and yearns for forgiveness.
Love only will endure in our fleeting world of flimsy wealth and health,
Love only will endure in our lives forever.

As I sit in meditation at Thy feet, I offer my love unto Thee.
Give me the grace to spread my love to all around
just like the lamp put on a stand.
Give me the strength to bear all things for the sake of love,
For Love Only Will Endure – L.O.W.E

18. Fidelity, Serenity, Eternity–we are in it together

To be faithful to someone or to some ideology is a difficult task.
But when we are faithful, we are living a part of that serene eternity.
The turbulence along the journey is temporary and
calmness will soon return.
The serenity that we feel is part of Thy eternity.

The times I have been unfaithful and faithless, I offer Thee O Master.
The times I have been selfish and arrogant, I give Thee O Divine.
The times I have been self-righteous and proud, I give them to Thee.
The times I have been lukewarm to the needs of others,
I present them to Thee.

Let me be Thy child, O Divine Master.
Hold and Lead me like a little child.
Let me experience the wonders of Thy Love and marvel at Thy
Wisdom
Let Your love shine through my serenity and lead me to eternity.

19. Stand up together

Let us stand up together and demand our rights.
Let us stand up together to perform our duties.
We can shape the future of our community, country and the world.
If we stand together, no one can put us down.

Stand up together for the belief in our right convictions.
Stand up together to help those in need.
Stand up together to change this world.
Stand up together to protect, preserve and persevere.

Stand up together to protect the weak,
Stand up together to protest against injustice,
Stand up together to bring about a fair distribution of wealth,
Stand up together to bring about peace.

20. The power of silence

The power of silence is stronger than the burst of loud talk.
In the silence of my heart, I can listen to my inner self with noise reduction.
Often I want to fill my life with noise to stifle the inner voice.
It is easier to listen to music than to listen to silence.

When I sit in deep silence at Thy feet, I feel calm and serene.
The surrounding noise I recognize for what it is.
I see myself immersed in the rhythmic dance that Thou art playing and watching.
I hear the sound of silence and see the dazzling dance.

Play Thy music through this silence that I experience,
Write Thy works with my hands,
Speak Thy words with my mouth,
Listen to Thy words with my ears.

Let the power of silence be the loudspeaker,
Let the power of silence be the inner voice,
Let the power of silence be the motivating factor,
Let the power of silence transform me.

21. Understanding – standing with U

O Divine, grant me the gift of understanding.

Help me to understand U and understand Thy revelation in all those around me.

I looked for U everywhere – in our places of worship, scriptures and prayers.

But where are U, O Divine?

Thou art everywhere, but I don't find Thee.

Thou art present here and now, I still search for Thee.

When I start understanding my brothers and sisters, I will understand U.

You are present in everything and in me... Reveal Thyself to me.

I meditate on the times that I did not understand U,

I recollect on the times when I did not understand my family, friends, colleagues,

I reflect on the times when I did not understand humanity and the environment,

Reveal Thyself to me O Master Divine.

Let me understand the mysteries of Thy creation,

Let me meditate on Thy love and compassion,

Let me understand the rhymes, rhythms and hymns that sing Your praises,

Let me understand U and stand with U always.

22. Water level

Like the water level, the needs of the world are often buried underneath.
The trickledown effect has yet to take place so that it percolates to some level of equality,
Water would always keep the water levels,
But our lives have not been like that, often resisting change.

Many rich people of the world are afraid to share their wealth …
A millionaire won't be a millionaire sans just one dollar…
But the millions mean zeroes on my death bed…
You have made me from Zero to Hero to Zero.

A new life is about to begin and I reflect on the days past.
As I near the end of my life I feel sorry for the wrong priorities that I had set.
I will not waste any more precious moments of my life.
I will share what I have with those in need.

Let me keep up the spirit of sharing and caring and
allow it to spring forth in me.
Let the desire for change arise within me like creative wellsprings,
Let the waters of justice and fairness flow to where it is lacking,
Let the water level be maintained so that no one is thirsty.

23. No child should go hungry

I am ashamed that after so many years of progress
in our human consciousness,
After so many years of advancement in agriculture,
medicine and technology,
After rapid strides in the learning progress in all disciplines – arts or science,
There are children who go to bed hungry even today, everyday.

I am upset that this situation is continuing to exist.
I am concerned about the gap between the rich and the poor.
The social framework in many countries does not include the poor and the marginalized.
Why can't we share our wealth and build a global social safety net?
Why can't we come together to eradicate malnutrition among
the most vulnerable?

O Master, how many more innocents have to die before we end wars?
How many more children should go hungry before they are fed?
How many more children be victims of poverty and malnutrition,
before my consciousness can arise and start to act?

In the silence of this moment, I take a resolve to do all I can to help and improve the situation.
Let me find ways and means to ensure that no one goes hungry and thirsty.
Let this resolve be turned into action and let this day be the starting point to achieve the solution through a firm resolution.

24. Each one, Teach one

If each one takes the initiative to teach at least one person,
We can remove illiteracy from the face of the earth.
If each one shares some food with another, we can banish hunger.
If each one shares some money with another, we can banish poverty.

Many find themselves on the fringe of the society not because of their fault.
They have reached there because of society's failure or through the cracks in our societal systems,
It may be that there were smarter people, who knew the system too well to make and take it to their own advantage.
They called others losers and some were even left behind to sleep on the sidewalk on cold winter nights.

Each one, teach one and so reach out to help one another.
It is easy for me to write this and for anyone to teach or preach about this.
It is so hard to get into real and meaningful action.
But with Thy help O Divine Master we will improve,
we will change this world.

25. Globalization – Winning Together

The world is an interconnected system today.
The advancement of technology has made the connections possible.
The news and views in any part of the world is known to others instantly.
The social media, internet, phone, television and radio all play a significant role in bringing about this connection.

In a globalized world, there are many winners and losers,
Let me ensure that I will do my best to enable social justice and fairness.
In an interconnected world, nobody is on the periphery any more,
Everybody is on the centre stage.

In a globalized world, the stage, the actors and the scripts are all global
And the drama is globalization.
As the drama is played out, many actors come and go.
The curtain closes and then again the curtain opens to a different setting.
Let me find meaning in a globalized world.

Let me build bridges and not walls; let me not stand in the way of progress,
Let me ensure that people are treated fairly in this global scenario.
Let me make sure that people are not branded as losers and winners,
Let me do my best to win together in this globalized world.

Winning together makes everyone happy, peaceful and contented.

26. Win-Win

I reflect on how we can all win together despite all
the roadblocks that are there.
Is it necessary that some lose so that others win?

The minimum wage workers versus the maximum earning CEOs,
Bonuses going to a few where the bar is raised
so high that many lose their share,
These are all strategies that are set up to step up the win-lose game,
There are many schemes being played out so that some win and
others lose.

The greed of humanity is evident in everything that we see,
the need for humanity to be served is there for everyone to see.
As long as we are guided by selfish interests and greedy people,
our society is going to limp along… and not prosper.

Let there be genuine leaders who are interested in the welfare of the
people,
let there be rulers who lead by example.
Let there be leaders who are willing to give up corruption,
let there be rulers who are able to sustain the environment and
govern.

27. What cannot be said in words

O Divine ... what words can describe Thee?
Thou art beyond the grasp of my little brain.
The rain, brain, grain all drain into Thee.
Everything points unto Thee.

As I journey on my human sojourn,
I fall and wound myself through my thoughts, words and actions.
I have hurt other people in many ways... forgive me for that.
All my thoughts, words and actions in the past cannot be undone.
They are written on the stone of history marching towards eternity.
I will be careful about my conduct in the future.

I will sit in silence and awe and watch Thy handiworks...
Thou art the Master and I am the student.
I am eagerly waiting for Thy mentoring lessons.
Words cannot describe, thoughts cannot imagine, actions cannot grasp Thee in Your Fullness.
So I think about Thy love, recite Thy name and sit in silent meditation adoring Thee.
Guard my thoughts, words and actions so that they may be pleasing to Thee.

In the silence of my heart, I internalize Thee and Thy love for me.
Though I am a fragile pot of clay, guard and keep me in Thy care.
Though I am weak in so many segments of my life,
keep me in Thy safe custody.
All that I am, I am offering to Thee as a fragrant offering and sing Thy fragrant serenade forever.

28. Like a shooting star

Like a shooting star, you came into my life.
Why do you move so fast and reveal Thyself only for a short while?
Hide not your countenance from me, O Master.
Let Thy radiance not blind me so that I cannot see you.

Stay in my life, O Beautiful One,
do not say goodbye to me.
I long for Thy company and love,
let me enjoy these moments with Thee.

When You are with me, the time stays still like Infinity,
my mind and heart rejoices in your company.
My thoughts are concentrated on you,
let me grab this moment and relish it in perpetuity.

29. Just One more touch Lord!

Just one more touch Lord, and I'll be clean again.
Just one more touch Lord, let me be Thy child again.
From the depths of my soul a cry arises; just one more touch Lord.
Just one more touch Lord and I'll be whole again.

When I feel your loving touch, my crisis is resolved.
I strayed from your circle of love and wandered in
the wilderness and darkness.
I dreamed of returning to your circle of love but something kept me away.
The pressures and the pleasures of life kept me away from Thee.
Now I return to Thy warm embrace with a promise never to
wander away from Thee.

Your love is enough for me…
Your words are the only ones that I need to hear.
Your books are the only ones that I need to read.
Such is Thy wisdom and knowledge, O Divine.

Reach out and touch me and let me be Thy child again!
Cleanse me of my past sins and let me start a new life again!
Wash me and purify my thoughts, words and actions.
Just one more touch, O Master, and I will be Thy child again.

30. Trimming our differences

Marching we will go ahead, trimming our differences,
Together we will build a peaceful home, community, country and a world.
Let the force of this union churn us to produce the best in us.
Let the differences melt away like snow with the warmth of friendship.

Human progress is hampered by concentrating on the differences.
So let me concentrate on all that is uniting us.
Let the walls of discrimination, regionalism and partiality crumble.
Let me focus on trimming our differences to march forward.

Our past has been marred by quarrels to settle scores.
Guns and violence determined the winners.
Let us commit ourselves to peace to win a serene and peaceful world.
For this is our aim and marching we will go ahead, trimming our differences.

31. Play Thy music in me

O Divine Master,
Play Thy music in me and let me leap with joy
For Thou art the player and I am the instrument.
Tune me so that I produce better sounds,
For Thou art the gardener and I am the plant,
Prune me so that I produce better fruits.

Thou art the weaver and I am the cloth
Weave a wonderful pattern out of me.
Thou art the Artist and the Architect,
Chisel a marvellous carving out of me.

When the strings break, replace them with fresh ones.
When the sounds crack, tune my voice.
When the ears don't hear, turn and amplify Thy voice.
When the eyes don't see, open them up to Your love.

32. The spark of the Divine…

The spark of the Divine is the starting force for the engine of my life
Let me have a contact with that Divine spark.
Being in Thy presence is the fuel which helps me to go forward.
Let the sparks give rise to flames of love to change and inspire.

My battery has been drained and now I need a boost.
Let Thy spark ignite the engine and while
I live my life my battery can recharge,
Let Thy spark be the start of a long journey of love,
Let Thy spark be the countdown to my ascent to Thee.

A single light left on in the vehicle can drain the battery
A single loophole in my life takes away my peace and serenity.
I need the spark of the Divine now,
To start again and go on my way to do Thy will.

33. Gravity, relativity, connectivity, creativity…

Let me reduce the chatter and listen to the creative mind
Science is evolving…
History is evolving…
Attitudes are evolving…
Humanity is evolving…
When will this evolution end or is it an endless process?

Our treatment of Mother Nature is important as we are all conjoined twins…
We are all interconnected.
Our race is only a three-legged race,
In which we have to synchronize and pull forward together.

We learn many things through association.
When we learn new languages, we associate words with the language we already know.
We associate movements with a stationary reference.
Similarly we need a reference point for our lives.

May You be that reference point in my life.
Let my universe revolve around Thee.
Let Thy love be the gravity that keeps me grounded,
Let Thy glory be the creativity,
Let Thy omniscience be the connectivity,
Let Thy greatness be the relativity that shows my dependence on Thee.

34. Negativity to Positivity

Negative thinking can have a destructive impact on me.
It can create a toxic work environment.
Many circumstances have made me play the victim card for far too long.
Let the positive thoughts flow into my brain now.

Envy, jealousy and all its friends show up at the door now and then,
Asking for accommodation in my heart and mind.
Let me chase them out of my being as they will ruin my life.
It is good to bring in positivity into my life.

Negative thinking has brought me to the shore of despair,
Constantly pushing me on to comparisons with others.
Positive thinking concentrates on cooperation and collaboration,
Negative thinking concentrates more on gloom and doom.

Let me live my life without comparing it with others,
As the comparison will only bring in more negativity into my life.
Every comparison reduces the appreciation that I should have for others,
Every comparison reduces the fullness that I can achieve in my life.

35. The attitude of gratitude...

The attitude of gratitude is the best attitude we can have in our life.

"Where are the other nine?" Jesus asked the one who returned to thank him. He was one out of the ten lepers who were cleansed...

So it's good to nurture an attitude of gratitude to our parents, teachers, managers, superiors, colleagues, friends and acquaintances.

Take the time in our life to say "Thank You" to all those who have helped us to become who we are.

Do not delay as it may be too late to thank them when you want to.

The cultivation of this attitude is not for its own sake.

It brings together other virtues along with it – empathy, compassion, sharing, caring are just some of them.

Evolution of mankind will be on attitude more than the mutation of genes or physical traits.

Let this attitudinal transformation begin with me.

For some persons, the other person is only seen as an object to be used.

The interactions border on "will to power" and team members, colleagues and friends are slaughtered by the sword of this "ego".

The need to cultivate a grateful heart is as important as our life itself.

A life devoid of a grateful attitude is a greedy, shallow and hollow life.

Think...think... Thank.

36. Cogito ergo sum

I think of the day when "I think, therefore I am" was coined
by René Descartes.
Is my thinking self alone that makes my whole being?
I am beyond my thinking self.
Even when I think I have rationally grasped everything,
something is missing.
What is this missing link?

Aristotle defined man as a rational being.
I think of the times when my ego was hurt,
When my ego was responding to situations.
I think of the times when my emotions ruled my behaviour.

Let me ask proper questions at all stages in my life.
I am emotional, therefore I will think…
Let my thinking set me apart,
Let that thinking make me a balanced person with wonderful
thoughts and emotions.

37. Time and Money

Time is more important than money against the backdrop of eternity.

Money is more important against the backdrop of my needs and wants.

Constantly there is a longing in me to acquire more assets, money and power.

Is my time being utilized fully well?

I learn about the time value of money and realize that a dollar today is worth more than a dollar tomorrow.

I don't learn about the money value of time well spent.

I also know that the time that I spend with my family and community is important.

Both seem to be diametrically opposed to each other.
One squeezes the other.

Work-life balance always hangs in a balance.

At the end of the battles for money and power,
I find an empty life that is not fully lived.

I think of the years I have wasted running after money,

when it should have been for my family, friends and community.

On my deathbed, what would give me more satisfaction – a life well lived or a life spent running after fleeting things and pleasures…

I deeply meditate on time and money
as they are determining attributes of my life.
My life will depend on how I control them and
which one becomes the primary key.
If money and power control me, my life is futile and the beautiful
outcomes of my life cannot be retrieved in its entirety.

So help me O Divine Master to value both time and money
with the proper perspective.
Let me not go after money and power
but go after things that will be beautiful ever after.

38. To exist is to coexist

"To exist is to coexist," was a famous saying of Gabriel Marcel.
To coexist with You is my daily dream.
How beautiful is it to sit at Thy feet and praise you all the days of my life.
Not mine, but Thy will be done.

These days countries are often at odds with each other,
Communities and persons are in competition with one another.
The peaceful co-existence remains only on paper.
So much of jealousy and envy make a scar and scare us.

Just as Nations form geographical blocks,
Individuals join together to form groups.
Some of these groups are just to put down others…
Why do we not see everyone and everything as one…

The success of my neighbour should not cause jealousy or envy,
The snobbish attitude and arrogance won't help us to grow.
Let us put aside the ego that prevents us from appreciating others,
Instead see that there can be inner peace only
when we have won the war on ego.

39. You are immortal

From the heights of Everest mountain,
From the depths of the Pacific ocean,
I will cry out with joy about You.
You are immortal; you will be remembered for ever.

Your words and deeds have left a deep impression upon me.
You will ever be remembered every day of my life.
You were the light house for my sailing ship,
You are immortal; you will be remembered till the end of all ages.

Your actions were a beacon to me,
Your words were so soothing and mild.
Your smiles encouraged me to be good,
You are immortal; you are my friend forever and
will be honoured in perpetuity.

40. Food banks and Swiss banks

The Food banks hold food for the poor and needy.

The Swiss banks hold the money for the rich and the elite.

It is okay to be rich and to make money, but it's a duty for our collective human consciousness to ensure that no one goes to bed hungry.

This should be a joint effort by all countries.

While millions suffer from famine and hunger all over the world, millions throw away their extra food in garbage bags that end up in landfills.

As inflation inflates the prices, a section of the society would be constantly pushed down the economic ladder,

Speculators drive up the prices of essential commodities like oil and constantly shake up the economic ladder.

The volatility of the stock markets makes them shock markets and as a result a few become rich but many lose out.

It's like a merry-go-round except that we don't know when it reaches the bottom or the top and when the fall by gravity starts and when the resistance finally takes effect.

For this reason, let us resolve to do our best to rid the world of hunger,

Even if others don't act, let us do something about it.

Even if we are not successful, we can do our best.

Food banks are the need of the hour and
no one should go hungry in our age.

41. Spring after the Winter

We should not lose hope as there is always a spring after the winter.
There is life and death as death gives way to life.
When everything seems ended in winter, there springs the Spring with new leaves on every tree.

There comes a fast before the feast,
A Good Friday comes before an Easter,
A suffering comes before joy,
A death comes before eternal life.

Winter is so cold and tough,
Spring is so lively and hopeful,
Summer is full of joy,
Autumn is full of waiting for the winter so that a spring can come after it.

42. One World, One Dream

We belong to One World with One Dream.

We belong to the same family and our dream is that everyone succeeds.

Through networking and social media,
the whole world has become a global village

and everything is within the reach of everyone.

Time and space has just shrunk so much…

We are just a click away…

Let our dreams fill the entire world,
Let our hopes lift the entire spirit,
Let our joy brighten things up,
Let our love transform the world to be One.

In this One world of interconnectedness,
Let us dream that our future is bright.
Where we can all pull together to win together,
And make this world a better place to live in.

43. The common human consciousness

The common human consciousness is waiting to be heard,
It is the sentinel of our future growth.
To make progress on our common destiny,
We are in it together.

The universal love radiates in each one of us.
It is this love that makes us brothers and sisters.
We have to stop the bloodshed in the name of religion, culture, politics or anything else.
Violence has no place in our hearts.

Let the human consciousness arise in our hearts,
To give way to all the temptations and tribulations,
Let our society move towards more compassion and love,
Let the forces of evil melt away and
allow the human consciousness to emerge.

44. The two solitudes

There is a saint and a sinner,
A stoic and an epicurean in me.
I do the things that I don't want to do,
And I am lazy to do the things that I should do.

I procrastinate …
I am constantly fighting these types of two solitudes every time.
I am having a duel with these dual forces every day.

When I want to be good, the bad things I wanted to avoid just happen,
Why is this dichotomy in my life?
Let me be aware of these dual solitudes in my life,
Let me make careful choices at all times.

45. Useless quarrels

I reflect on the trivial and useless quarrels that I spend my time on.
It does not help me to grow any better but just boosts
my ego in trying to prove a point.
I was adamant and held fast onto my position with unwavering strength,
But I feel defeated now. What happened to my inflated ego?

Useless quarrels end uselessly wasting my precious time
Action and reaction are natural impulses.
Action and proper reaction are divine impulses.
Useless quarrels are not worth the while.

The quarrels don't make me grow,
The quarrels make me come to blows.
Let my thoughts rise up and focus on Eternity,
The rise of the ego is the fall of Divinity.

I am resolved to avoid unnecessary quarrels
And support each other with loving praise
For it is in this harmony
That our life's potential can be fulfilled.

46. The robins will sing again

The winter will go and the spring will come,
The robins will sing again.
The Good Fridays will go and Easter will come.
We will sing again "Halleluiah!"

War will go and peace will come
We will sing again "Shalom!"
Hunger will go and food will come
We will be satisfied again.

Greed will go and contentment will come
We will be happy again.
Pain will go and relief will come
We will be singing again.

47. Dream with me

Dream with me to create a better world.
Let our dreams flow like streams through the barren land of despair.
Let the land be nourished by the refreshing water, cherished for a long time.
Let our imagination reach out to the skies.

We will innovate and build a better place,
We will change all that needs to be changed.
We will fix all that needs to be fixed,
We will make our dreams come true.

Dream with us to make poverty a legend of the past
    to make education a reality,
    to bring about a fairer world.
Dream with us to go beyond our dreams and act.
Inspire and help one another to go beyond our limitations.
Dream for a better tomorrow that all of us may live happy, contented and peaceful lives.

48. Discrimination

We have seen discrimination ever since our birth.
Discriminations institutionalized and instituted by groups of people, often in some form of power and influence.

I see the genocides in Rwanda and Darfur,
I hear and learn about the holocaust,
I see a documentary on Albinos being mutilated in Tanzania,
I hear about the struggle of the common man protesting in the streets against their oppressors
Trying to break the glass ceilings placed as rules, regulations, policies, procedures etc…

The secret partialities and discriminations have to end one day,
So that everyone has an equal opportunity at the start of the race.
The winner is decided and rewarded considering how well the person ran and not by any other factor.
The outcome is not decided at the beginning of the race itself.

It's human intelligence which has helped us to survive as a species for so many years.
Should this not continue to help us make our life a little better?
But when this universal intelligence is tampered with, a mythical kingdom ruled by paranoid rulers create an unjust ecosystem where the rights of others are forgotten.
No society is immune to this problem.

49. Drench me in Thy love

My heart has become an arid zone,
drench me in Thy Love.
My mind has become a barren desert,
drench me in Thy Love.

My head has become heavy laden,
keep me in Thy Love.
My hands have become inactive,
keep me in Thy Love.

My feet are tired of walking,
help me to face all these difficulties.
My body is aching,
help me to continue walking without fear.

My habits have become unbearable, help me overcome the routine.
My thoughts have become empty and my actions meaningless,
help me to find meaning in meaningless situations.

50. Divine Melody

Every time I listen to a tune the truth dawns on me and
every music piece points to a perfect bliss and harmony.
The mind unconsciously dwells on the eternal tunes
that is divine melody to my ears.

Play Thy loving melody so that I can peacefully fall asleep
listening to Thy music.
Send Thy gentle wind to caress me so that I can peacefully fall asleep
experiencing Thy touch.

Give me the grace to forgive so that I can peacefully live
seeing Thy epiphany in all that is there to see.
Give me the strength to bear every pain that comes along
as without this pain, I may not gain much in my life.

51. The Awakening…

When will my selfish self be awakened to the reality of eternity?
When will I realize my futile rush after earthly things?
When will my Being be awakened to its true nature?
When will I see the fertile land promised beyond earthly things?

When will I shed my ego and transcend to the reality of eternity?
When will I feed my brothers and sisters to quench their hunger and thirst?
When will I sit in meditation and realize my true self?
When will I see that promised land?

When will I become more humble and simple?
When will I become more helpful and loving?
When will I become more generous and courteous?
When will I see that promised land?

52. Beyond my thinking silos

I have been conditioned to think that all that I think is the reality.

But instead the reality that I perceive is conditioned by my thinking.

My conditioned brain made me perceive the world with a coloured glass of selective perception,

Often with prejudice, partiality and discrimination.

I have been selective in my dealings with friends, neighbours and relatives.

Sometimes I have been conditioned by my thinking silos to divide people.

I have chosen my friends and my enemies,
conditioned by my prejudiced thinking.

Help me to remove these filters.

Let me remove the coloured glasses,

Let me remove the generalizations,

Let me remove all that blocks my vision of Reality.

53. Right and wrong

Today I ponder on what is right and wrong.
The rules that are set forth are not carved in stone.
The rules are for us and not we for the rules.
Many dictators, demagogues and a few politicians make rules for others
Extolling its goodness but never having to follow them.
They always have a loophole that they could make use of.

Rules which are discriminatory have to go one day or another.
The whole world is changing and the rules will have to change.
The human species evolved over time to this point in history...
Many righteous people had to give up their freedom and lives to uphold our freedom and lives.
They sacrificed their lives for us.

Some persons and organizations do not want to change.
Every change brings in pain and causes some disturbance to the established norms, beliefs and structures.
Hence the hierarchy often prefers to procrastinate or put down the legitimate aspirations of its people and maintain the status quo.
As the time changes so too our rules should change,
We always interpret things and events against the background of current beliefs.
We need to accommodate our common growth aspirations and progress in our evolutionary consciousness.

54. All are my brothers and sisters

In many pledges that I have made,
I mentioned about treating everyone as my brother and sister.
But I have not lived up to that expectation.
I looked at people with coloured glasses so that I can fit them into some pre-conceived notions.

Stereotypes generalized by culture, religion,
nationality, ethnicity,
colour, language etc.
These are all just accidents and not the substance of our being.
Help me O Master to follow the substance and
not the fleeting skin deep values.

Everyone needs to be treated with genuine respect, concern and love,
Everyone has a right to live in freedom and dignity, without ever having to feel marginalized by any of his or her attributes.

55. Eat to live

I have heard of the maxim, “Eat to live and not live to eat.”
But have I lived up to it?
Often I have gone beyond what I needed.
When so many go to bed hungry and weary,
I sleep comfortably between my clean sheets.
When will I learn to care,
    dare to share,
    care to share?

The world has sufficient resources for everyone.
Mahatma Gandhi once said, “There is sufficient for everyone’s need,
not for everyone’s greed ”.
Help me to think of all those who are without food
    and other amenities of life
    and dedicate a portion of my earnings and time for them.

56. Stillness for Wellness

Stop my wandering mind,
keep it still so that I can discover all Thy Glory in that stillness.
In that stillness of eternity, I will gladly live my life.

I am so busy browsing the internet,
Checking the volatile stock markets,
Monitoring the ever changing exchange rates,
But I fail to take stock of my present condition.

Connectivity seems so important that I cannot even
    disconnect from the social networking sites until I am tired.
    I disconnect and with a sigh of relief my mind resets and rests.
I like to tweet on twitter the whole day,
I tweet what I feel; I feel what I tweet; I am what I tweet.

Though a limited and proper use of these can be useful to me,
I have almost become addicted to them.
I give into small temptations without considering the consequences
And forget about the stillness that is needed for my wellness.

Help me O Divine, to keep away from things that make me fall.
If I fall, give me the courage to pick myself up and
start walking straight again.
Sitting in the silence of this moment, my brain is writing a thousand
research papers; my brain is drawing roadmaps of ambitions.

Help me to be still… Let me look in the water to see myself.
Let me look into the mirror to see my real self.
Let me not keep on thinking and find that I am still thinking and failing to fall asleep.
Let the crescendo arise in the wellness of stillness.

I have been shifting the goal posts so often that no goals are scored even though the game is on...
Keep my mind and heart focused on Thee.
Give me stillness for my wellness.

57. God did His homework day before yesterday…

Today I reflect on the Infinite, the Omnipotent and the Omniscient Power.

How small are we, when we think of the vastness of the Infinite.

The attributes from my lips, from my mind, from all the books,

Cannot be sufficient to describe Thee, O Divine.

The Divine draws straight lines through crooked curves.

When I look at my life and ponder on all those things that have happened,

I see a straight line, drawn with crooked curves.

Let Thy Intelligence be my guiding thought.

My little brain fails to understand Thy Depth,

  Thy Length,

  Thy Width,

  Thy Height.

Thy volume and area are just beyond my grasp and I long to be with Thee.

58. Pearls

Pearls are formed by irritants that enter the oyster
and this metamorphosis is a lesson to be learnt.
Your rays from the sun become golden beams on the clouds,
and on the snow-clad mountains which give us joy.

Spread your radiant rays in my life.
Let my life beam with joy, for Thou art shining within me.
Let me reflect that radiance back to my brothers and sisters.
Let me turn all my present troubles into "pearls" of joy,
peace and achievement.

The pearls of patience will surely pay off one day.
A change of heart is all I need to be a pearl.
Let all the mistakes, failures, trials and tribulations in my life
be transformed into precious pearls in my life.

59. Enlightenment

I am going through an inner awakening.
I want to see Thee.
Eternal is Thy Life,
Omniscience is Thy Knowledge,
Omnipotence is Thy Power.
I bow in humble adoration before Thee.

I have been a rebel, but the decibel of the noise is coming down.
Thou hast shown me the path.
Enlightenment happens to those willing to listen,
    those willing to understand,
    those willing to see,
    those willing to hear and interpret,
    those willing to go beyond and believe.

60. The moment of truth

Very often we are afraid to speak the truth because it can hurt,
Truth is not liked by many who want it to be hidden.
It is not easy to be on the side of truth
when the rewards are many on the other side,
It is not easy to be on the side of truth when truth has been morphed.

Truth has been diluted to grey areas, distorted by time and place.
Truth has been absent from many social networking and media reporting,
Truth has been missing in many of our words and actions,
Truth has been lacking in our longing to do good for others.

To face the truth is a difficult thing.
Many a time have I failed to speak and stand up for truth.
It's easy to cheat a person or the system
but I am cheating myself in the whole game.
Shooting self-goals will lead to unending loss and failure.

A small gain for fame or wealth is what motivates many of us to be adversaries of truth.
This is so fleeting but we prefer to take sides with what is untrue.
Corruption has gripped the society like a cancer
that can end our existence in harmony,
We need to really remove this cancer to survive as a free society.

Let me commit myself to be on the side of truth and hope.
Let me become a beacon of hope,
champion of truth even in the midst of adversity.

61. The pressures of life

The pressures of life led me to the pleasures of life.
But now I realize my folly and I want to return to Thee.
Like the prodigal son, I come back to Thee.
Many elder sons point a finger against me and prevent my entry.

Many elder sons expect me to continue to be a prodigal
so that they get the full share of the father.
Many elder sons expect me not to return
so that the family and community name is preserved.

I am sorry that my life has been like that of the prodigal son,
but now I am returning to Thee.
I can see you waiting for me with open arms,
let me run into Thy warm embrace.

Let no elder son stop me from stepping into Thy house,
You are my Father too.
I have ruined Your name, my name
but You are a forgiving Father happy at my return.

Allow me to step into Thy house and let me rest a while,
I promise not to go astray any longer.
Your love and affection are sufficient for me to live,
To lead kinder and stronger lives.

Do not turn me away to go back to my old ways,
do not allow me to be derided by the elder brothers,
do not allow me to be rejected by the tribe,
do not throw me away from Thy love and care.

Accept this prodigal son and let me always stay close to you,
Abide in your love and never go astray.

62. Please don't say goodbye

My parents, teachers, relatives, family and friends are saying good-bye to me,

One by one they disappear.

I feel part of my Being is being diminished with their passing.

But I am called upon to live my life to the fullest under all circumstances.

As I hold on to my ageing parents,

As I hold the shivering hands of a dying patient,

I say, "Please don't say good bye".

Your life was a beacon of light,

Your love was as cozy as a glove,

Your intentions were without pretensions,

Your life was full of caring and sharing.

Let me salute thy earthly sojourn,

I know that one day when we escape the gravitational force of death,

We will all enter into the outer space of eternity without any more effect of the gravity of sin.

Until then I will remember all your prayers, love, care and concern for me.

Let that be a motivating factor for me to live my life fully.

I mentally place these flowers, gifts and awards in your hands,

Please accept them as a token of my heartfelt gratitude.

You are immortal ....you will live in my heart forever.

I will see you there sooner than later. Just wait for me!

63. The eternal silence

I sit in silence, I want to be still.
I am silent but a thousand voices are shouting inside me.
Let me shut out all that has happened today…
Let me close my conversation to myself in my brain…

Silence can speak louder than words.
This is what the mystics,
    sages,
    saints,
    And many other spiritualties have taught us.

Silence….
I become aware of my breathing.
It is the living breath that sustains me.
My life is sustained by everything around me including
    the air that I breathe,
    the water that I drink,
    and the food that I consume.
Let me enjoy this silence around me as that represents a glimpse of eternity.

64. Crisis – the cry rises

I reflect on whether I am going through a crisis,
If not, I think of someone who is going through a crisis.
I can be affected by a crisis at any time.
A crisis can be a blessing and need not be a curse.

All my attachments, illusions, conditioning cause my suffering.
My suffering is simply a resistance to reality.
A crisis is a time of reflection for me.
Though it inflicts pain, I want to see it as an opportunity for change.

While I undergo this crisis, a deep cry rises within me.
Let me come out of this crisis victorious.
Through the pain, rejection and sadness I feel now,
Let me transform them and make them into pearls of joy.

65. Growth

I stand on the weighing balance to see the extra weight I have gained.
Let me stand in front of the mirror and examine myself.
I want to see if my company,
my community,
my country,
and the whole world is growing.

While billions are stashed away in offshore secret accounts,
millions are pushed away to suffer hunger and malnutrition silently.
Millions don't understand that it is their sacred duty,
to pull along these people to a life of decency worthy of human existence.
Let us arise, let our consciousness arise and include everyone
in our march towards growth.
Until then growth remains a distant mirage.

66. The one dollar bill

Let us ponder and reflect on the one dollar bill now.
Let it speak to us about its life story.

When we listen to the story, it would amaze us.
It has moved through the hands of the rich and the poor.
It has moved through the collection baskets of the church and all religious functions.
They have been used in bribing, paying school tuition fees, to purchase lifesaving medicines…
The one dollar bill is a symbol of what every currency bill goes through every day.

After I was delivered from the Security press where I was born,
    I went as a tip into a bartender's cup,
    The stationery store,
    The church donation basket,
    At the toll station,
    As tips in clubs, restaurants and then
    Into the hat of a homeless person.
    I have visited the food cart that sold some hot coffee,
    To the wallet of a person where I stayed for a number of months,
    To the school campaign for free dress day,
    To fast food restaurants and big chain stores,
    And now my journey is still continuing on…
You can imagine the rest of my journey

as I am now embedded into your mind.

Pray that I may be used for the best of things until I am useful no more.

My value is one dollar now and as time goes on

My value will be diminished,

until no one accepts me any longer.

It will be time for me to give way for a new bill which will continue my journey and see similar places until it's time for it also to move on…

On the one dollar bill is written the words – In God we trust.

The trust between people have been taken beyond to the power of the Divine.

The trust between people can be broken, trust between friends and family can be broken;

But the trust with God or the Divine cannot be broken.

It is an everlasting covenant bonded beyond the ups and downs of this world.

No recession or depression can rescind this trust in the Divine.

No socio-economic reality can reduce the trust in Thee O Divine Master.

We live in the Divine and the Divine lives in us.

67. Judge Not

We are in a hurry to judge others and there is reminder everywhere that we should not judge.
But constantly I judge others and pass my judgment.
The context in which I judge others is often wrong.

When I have a speck in my eye
Why am I hurrying to condemn my neighbour?
The judgmental behaviour is all too common around us.
What we don't understand is that the actions of persons are conditioned by the circumstances which constantly change and the gene which communicates hereditary traits.
It is easy for us to bottle people into generalized capsules according to our perceptions.
Visionaries and prophets have told us that people should not be judged as sinners,
underprivileged, underdogs or any other classification.
The saints could be even worse sinners, if they had the same circumstances as those who are sinners.
Pope Francis has set a great example by asking, "Who am I to judge?"
Let us resolve not to judge people.

68. The curtain has been raised

The curtain has been raised on my life.
I have to act and everyone is watching.
I do not want to exit the scene without giving my contribution.
The Director is watching...
The prompter is prompting...
But I have to act.

Neither the director nor the prompter comes on stage...
I have to fulfil my role for the drama to be complete.
Let me play my role.
O Divine, You are the Director
    You decide my entry and exit time.
    Let me make good use of the opportunity.
    Let me accomplish my role to the best of my ability.
    The rest I leave unto Thee.

69. The Zen Buddha

The Zen Buddha stage is that stage of life
When I realize the human consciousness,
When I see the folly of chasing earthly goods and pleasures,
When I can see the part in the whole,
When I can see the bigger picture against the backdrop of eternity.

The time, places and events should not drag me down.
We have to synergise the energy of our colleagues.
Let me not give myself to inaction and empty chatter,
Let me give myself to proactive thinking and peaceful action.

Let there be a peaceful state of mind with contentment,
The natural state of our consciousness,
The perfect acceptance of our corporal bodies with all its limitations,
These are all pointing to a Zen Buddha stage.

70. Falling and rising again

Every child learns to walk by falling.
They fall, rise and walk again.
It is the courage and simplicity that makes the children walk.
It is this courage that we need to rise again when we fall.

Human Nature is a combination of success and failure.
Every student has failed the expectations of his parents, teachers or someone else at some time in his life.
Every company has failed to meet the expectation of the analysts, shareholders or employees at some time in its existence.
Every person has failed or lost something in his or her life.

It is natural that people lose and win,
It is natural that companies go bankrupt,
It is natural that persons go into periods of failure and oblivion,
It is also natural that all these could rise up from their ashes…

Many a time, we become victims of the power and ego game,
Those who have control over others like to play this game without knowing the impact.
The "will to power" is what motivates them.
But let us not get discouraged by these events
Let's rise and walk again.

71. Time and timing

Timeless time,
Every moment of every day,
Don't waste time,
Compare it with eternity and infinity.

I fail on time management,
At the end of the day, a chasm of emptiness is all I have got.
Let me chart out my time properly,
As the seconds and minutes pass by,
Let me not watch it pass by silently.
Let me make the best use of every second,
  every minute
  every hour,
  every day,
  every month,
  every year,
So that my entire life can be a wonderful and fragrant offering unto Thee.
I will sing a fragrant serenade unto Thee forever.

72. Eternal Intelligence

Ice – Water – Vapour,
Solid – Liquid – Gas,
The distant galaxies millions of light years away…
The food chain rhythm…
Let Thy eternal intelligence flow through my heart and mind.

I have not scratched the surface of Thy eternal intelligence manifested through Thy wonderful creation.
I am amazed by Thy Glorious deeds,
I am bathed in Thy showers of blessings.
I marvel at Thy wonderful love.

Wonderful designs – greater than the best design pattern,
Excellent balance – better than the best acrobat,
Tremendous sights – better than the best visualization,
Precision rhythm – better than the most precise watch.
Let me be marvelled by Thy Eternal Intelligence.

73. Free to be free

Let us reflect on freedom today…

What is freedom and how is freedom understood?

It is true that we are not fully free to be free in today's world.

In many places in the world today,

people's destiny is being stage managed by a small group,
who want to have control and power over others.

Some regimes restrain the freedom of their people so that they rule like Kings of old.

They retain full control over people's lives and treat them without respect.

Democracies sometime limit the freedom of people just for the sake of achieving the limited power ambitions of a few people or groups.

They solemnly attribute these restraints to the growth of religion, language, culture, nationality or other reasons…

Persecution in the name of preservation is still persecution unacceptable.

These are dangerous interventions limiting our growth.

Let us resolve to become active catalysts causing change for the better.

74. Riches

Wealth and fame, I sought
Like many others I played the game of growth in business, property, stocks, career, bank balance and assets of various portfolios.
With a selfish motive, I played the game
often not caring for others around me.
The "me first" attitude has given me an instinct for
unrestrained competition with my co-workers and friends.
"What's in it for me?" has created an unhealthy competition where I have not been allowing others also to grow.

I thought I would be happy as a local chieftain,
owning land, buildings, jewellery.
But now I am looking beyond riches and career,
which only satisfies me temporarily.
I realize that life is a game to be played fairly.

The day will come when I will have to leave and so I am interested in permanent treasures.
What will be my legacy – riches which can be traded or permanent riches?
I realize that the choice is mine.
Let me consciously choose everything that is permanent.

75. The joy of losing

Recollect the anger that you feel when you lose the game,
Remember the time you lost face in an embarrassing situation.
Recall the time a partner ditched you,
Remember the time your boss sidelined you,
prevented you from growing,
for some unknown motive.
These are just temporary wins for them,
There is a joy of losing when you think beyond the moment.
It is better to lose a small fight and win a war later.
Small fights don't determine destiny or legacy,
They are not worth your fight.

Let us concentrate on the positive energy that can overcome
the sorrow that is experienced at the moment.
Let the ego take its retreat and let the sunshine of hope, joy and peace arise.
Let all negative thoughts disappear even though
I have lost in something today,
Let all that is positive fill my being as tomorrow is a day full of opportunities.

76. We grow together... What's in it for me to us...

Constantly we ask, "What's in it for me?"
Our initiative to act is even dependent on this.
Why do we act this way?
It's because our human nature tends to be selfish.

But humans are completely different from all other species,
we are able to make rational decisions,
we have evolved over time to understand others.
Let not selfishness remove the sap from the trees of our life.
The ego and selfishness are the biggest hindrances in our personal growth.
Some take pleasure to make others fall
they perceive others as threats and competitors.
But there is sufficient space for all to achieve and shine.
Humans have this great ability to feel empathy;
When that is missing we have selfishness and ego
dictating terms to us.

Let me resolve today to make my life more selfless
so that collaboration, cooperation and limited competition
might help me grow.

77. Work in progress

I am a work in progress …

My birth to death is a journey of a couple of years,

My Life is a transformative process.

I am a living document which is being written and edited by so many…

Like the Wikipedia,

I am a collaborative project.

Thou art the Potter, I am the clay.

Thou art the Painter, I am the canvass.

Thou art the Giver and I am the receiver.

My life is a journey and I am determined to enjoy the journey.

Whatever be the difficulties on the way, I am determined to give my best.

Even if I fail and fall, I will rise again and return to you.

For You are the Master and the Builder and I am a work-in-progress.

78. Serendipity

I look at the synonyms for serendipity…
Chance, fate, destiny, karma, providence…

Is my life one of serendipity, deserving the pity of others?
No. I can change this "surrender pity".
I can fill my life with compassion, empathy, friendship and love.
I can shine forth like a candle that spreads light to all until it is burnt out.

I want to keep on burning so that others can see the light.
I want to keep on talking about things that really matter!
I want to keep on reading and writing about topics that are worth it.
I want to keep on working, helping, caring and sharing until the very end.

I want to turn my life around and ensure that its goals are met.
I want to ensure that my vision is clear,
I want to set clear goals,
I want to have the best strategies to achieve the goals.

79. Inspiration and perspiration

We do not live by perspiration alone, but by timely inspiration.

The inspiration is a creative gift endowed on us by the Divine.

The flow of the creative juices is a divine act

The conversion of that inspiration requires perspiration.

Every bit of human progress has been carved out
through inspiration and perspiration.

Every great activity requires this transaction of thought and action.
Our lives value is based on the level of actualization of our inspiration.

Let me resolve to be inspired,

Steadfast in the execution of this inspiration,

Committed to keeping up with this habit,

Resolute in our love for human progress,

Persistent to innovate new things and processes,

Dedicated to that passion for ever.

80. Light and shadow

Day and Night
Rain and Shine
Summer and winter
Mountain and Valley
...
Are you not all the opposites that create the one reality?
Your reason and season will never vanish.
I see only the shadow of Thy Light.
Lead me to the Light.

I am engulfed in a tinted glass effect of consciousness
That does not reveal the inner occupants.
Help me to discover and see who I really am.
Let me find my real self.
O Divine, the doors are unlocked for you to enter.
I want to open the windows to let the fresh air come in.
Your fragrant scent fills my body, soul and mind and
they dance for joy at Thy sight.
Accept me as a fragrant offering pleasing to Thee.

81. Quality pays and stays

Doing something is always better than doing nothing.
Doing that something with a stamp of quality is the best thing to do.
When I deliver things with quality a sense of satisfaction comes to me.
It says a lot about my personality.

Companies hire people who can deliver outcomes with quality.
People like others who can make a change in their lives with a positive quality,
This quality is all that we seek in others
So that they promote quality in all that they do.

Often the pressures of deadlines have made my deliverables lack the quality,
The transient nature of life reveals itself in some of my works.
Let me think of the times when I hurried and did not concentrate,
Let me focus on what I do with quality… for it will stay with me forever.

82. Life and its functions

Life is like modular programming with functions and subprograms.
When all the parts or modules work well, the whole life also works well.
Often it is some function or other that does not work well and it affects our entire life.
So it is necessary to fix that function or module for the full integrity of life to work together.

Many times it is external factors that make us worry and affect our lives,
The laws, customs, societal and social demands all put pressure on us.
Some of these could derail our lives,
And a few functions may malfunction.

Let me take a resolve to look at all that is troubling or worrying me now.
Let my life be examined and let me determine where I can improve,
Let my life become happy and contented once again.
Let all the modules in my life work harmoniously to bring joy and peace in my life.

83. The fast lane

I have tailgated and forced people to move out of the fast lane,
So that I reach the destination five minutes earlier.
I forgot all the while that we had a common destiny.
The five minutes I gained do not matter in the long run.

The road rage was not worth the fight,
It is patience, love, peace and joy which are more important, even if I am on the slow lane.
In a fast paced world of cut-throat competition,
These virtues are like oases for a traveller in the middle of a desert.

The stress that I have created,
The distress that I have caused,
The angst and strain that I have formed,
The anguish and torments that I have produced,
Defines my fast lane journey.

The fast lane may not be the best lane and virtue may travel in other lanes…
Let me understand that fast lane may not be the best for me always…
Let me not tailgate and push others to the side lane to save a few minutes…
Let me not sideline others into oblivion to score a few momentary goals…

84. The world and the Word

O Master, the world that we know today is beyond our comprehension
The words that we speak about Thee are beyond all understanding.
Words are one way of describing Thy wondrous Gifts,
Thy wisdom and love.
The denotations, connotations and hermeneutics of every word ultimately point to Thee.

Every prose and every poem speaks of Thy wonder,
All words and alphabets and pictures represent an eternal love for Thee.
We are waiting in hope and patience to be in communion with Thee.
Let the world that we create out of our words acknowledge Thee forever.

The world and the universe may pass and the words may change
But Thy love and wisdom will stay alive for ever.
We may discover new worlds similar to ours,
But Thy Words will stay alive for ever.

85. The meaning of meaning

O joyful Joy,
O happiest Happiness,
O peaceful Peace,
Thou art the meaning of Meaning.
The reason for my living, dying and living again.

This is the meaning of Meaning,
To find meaning in an apparently meaningless world.
To go beyond what I see,
To think beyond what I hear,
To dream beyond the present.

For many events in my life,
I cannot find any meaning now after so much of research.
But in five or ten years a better understanding evolves.
Help me to find meaning even when I grope in darkness.
Help me to find joy and peace even when I am back to the wall.

Guide me to the green pastures where I can find my repose,
Guide me from the difficult deserts to the soothing oases of peace, joy and love.
Let me find true meaning in Thy words,
Let me translate those words into action by doing the things that please You.

86. Best gift

The gift of life...

This is the best gift that I have ever received.

You woke me up from my eternal slumber

And placed a gift in my hand – the gift of my life.

I breathe in my blessings, joys, happiness…

And breath out my sins, failures, prejudices...

O Serenity come and transform my moment to eternity.

Serenity … Eternity… come and bring peace to this moment,

Ease... Peace... Peaceful.

O Joy come and transform this to a joyful moment,

Joy...joyful.

My life is a bouquet of flowers filled with various joys and sorrows,

Some are bright and others are not so bright,

But these flowers present the true reality of my nature.

All the virtues and sins, the joys and sorrows and so many other opposites,

Form the bouquet of my life and let me present them unto Thee.

I offer them as a fresh and fragrant offering to Thee acceptable in Thy sight.

87. The sunflower habit

Let me be like the sunflower that follows the Sun,
Let me follow You wherever you want me to move.
When the Sun sets, let me know that it will re-appear soon.
When the Sun rises, my heart fills with joy.

Your sunshine will keep me from harm and other distractions,
Your sunshine will help me survive,
Your sunshine gives me warmth,
As I see your movements, I change my direction.

Let Thy signals be signs in my life.
Let Thy design be the working plan for my actions.
Let me not turn away from Thy light and presence,
Let me be open to Thy grace and love.

88. My prayers and wishes

I prayed for riches, but you gave me work,
I prayed for wisdom, but you gave me understanding.
I prayed for peace but you gave me pain,
I prayed for love, but you gave me conflicts.

I bought the lottery, but my lot was to work again,
I prayed for prosperity, but you gave me poverty,
I prayed for my wishes, but you washed them away.
Why is my life a dichotomy of the opposites?

As I sit in silence meditating on my life so far,
I realize that my prayers have been the strength providers,
To accept a situation and find meaning and strength in it.
It encourages me to become better every day,
whatever my current situation is.

89. Death - the game changer

As soon as I was born, I was mature enough to die.
Will I go into an eternal state or be re-born to rectify my karma?
My time is almost over with no chance of overtime.
But I am happy looking at the report card.

You have given me good grades
You have overlooked my failing grades and averaged it all for me.
Thou art the Teacher, I am the student.
As my learning stops here on earth, let me look up to
You to yearn for the eternal bliss.

Death is the game changer in my life,
People and places; actions and functions; events and memories,
All these are being transformed along with me into eternity,
They are tagged as my attributes in some invisible file.

Let me accept death as an inevitable part of my transformation,
When this comes into my mind, my motivation becomes focused to be good.
Let me understand that with death, the game does not end,
It's the game changer forever.

90. In the Divine presence

In Thy Divine presence, I become aware of my breath,
I become aware of all other noises and shut them out.
In Thy presence, I stop my thinking.

Let me sit in Thy presence, O Almighty One.
I am only a part of your Whole,
I am the temple of the Divine.
It means, I need to respect everyone,
They also form the parts which make up the whole.

Every human being deserves respect,
No one deserves to live their lives in fear,
No one needs to live in hunger and tear,
Everyone is part of the Whole...everyone is part of the Divine.

As I sit in silent reflection at Thy feet,
Let me resolve to make this world a better spot,
Where everyone can live a decent life,
Where everyone works towards growth, peace and contentment.

91. NOW…enjoy the journey

Let me live my NOW and make it a joyful moment,
Let me enjoy the journey to my destination.
I do not know the actual time for the journey,
Whether there would be accidents on the way…
Let me enjoy the journey of Life.

If I squeeze from both sides - the actions of the past and worries of the future
I get NOW.
Let me live in the present.
So let me enjoy the journey of Life.

I was born in the PAST
I live in the PRESENT
And I will die in the FUTURE.
But let me enjoy the journey of Life NOW.

The time to act is NOW.
Tomorrow will have its own problems.
Let me contribute my best to alleviate the problems faced by others even in remote corners of the earth.
We are all an extended family.
The time to act is NOW and let's make it a peaceful and joyful moment!

92. Liberation from life's rut and maze

Today I reflect on my life's rut and the maze.
However much I try to get a handle on my life's problems, they elude me.
I am inhibited by my thoughts and actions of the past
that were not so positive.
The social media does not decrease my tension; actually it increases with the overuse of it.
I am addicted to it as if there is no escape.

My life is full of clutter and I want to organize my life.
I want to give heed only to positive thoughts for positive actions.
I search for the unsearchable but reach the earthly pleasures.
I get caught in a rut. Rut eventually turns into a kind of rust in my life,
Disfiguring the shine and brightness that I had in my life.
I want to break out of this rut … this is my resolve.

I want to avoid the situations that make me flare up.
Teach me forbearance with my family, relatives, friends,
colleagues, acquaintances etc.
You want to teach me something every day…
Teach me humility and let me live my life in simplicity and love.

93. Comparison impairs

Let me look at my plate and eat what I have,
When I look at my friend's plate, my satisfaction diminishes.
When I start comparing myself, my spouse, my children with others, it reduces my satisfaction;
Comparison really impairs when it is done without taking into consideration the unique value of everyone.

Let me do my best and leave the rest.
My natural instinct prompts me to compare me to others.
Often the result is only envy, jealousy and bitterness.
I do compare my children, friends, relatives, colleagues, bosses and superiors.
I conveniently forget that everyone is unique and are not given the same physical, emotional and intellectual capabilities.

Let me stop this habit of comparing myself or
others just to find fault and criticize.
Let me find ways to get motivated and to do better like
other successful people.
It needs a contented and enlightened person not to compare,
For it is the natural instinct to compare and play the victim.

94. Problems and onions

Why do I have a difficult boss, superior, spouse, teammate or teacher?
How would a pearl be made unless irritants are introduced?
Problems can melt away like the snow under the heat, if we expose our problems to the proper attitudes.
But how do I face all these problems?
Problems are like onions. When you feel them, they are big, but when you peel them, they disappear.

Let me concentrate on one of the problems that I have at the moment.
Genuinely, I want to become better and better.
But the demands and pressures of everyday life throw
my resolutions to the wind,
And I am back to square one.
Let me offer Thee O Divine, the problems and
I know that I can get a solution.

Let me turn all my current negative situations into positive ones.
I completely love and accept myself as I am with all my faults,
failures and talents.
Allow me not to fall again and again.
Let me walk with Thee in Thy presence,
That's enough for me as my problems melt in Thy sight.

95. The Trappist monk

I have heard of the Trappist monks,
who dig a little every day for their graves,
Reminding them that life is passing.
The end is clear and little acts serve as a means to
remind them about the end.

Teach me to concentrate on the eschatological values in my life.
Let me not run after fleeting pleasures and values.
When I am trapped in the existential pleasures of life,
Let me think of the Trappist Monks to give me the proper perspective.

I am trapped in looking for material welfare and instant gratification,
I am engulfed with amassing whatever I could as assets without any
consideration for others,
I am eager to please all my senses at all cost.
Help me not to be trapped in this instant material glory
but learn from the Trappist monks…

96. The passing

I am in the palliative care unit of the Hospital
  Living through my final days,
  Waiting for my final good bye.

"Expectation is greater than the event," they say.
My passing will come as if I go to sleep.
But this time, I will awaken to Thy eternal bliss.

I am happy with all that I have done, read, wrote, taught, achieved.
All other relevant verbs in their past tense, I offer thee.
I feel the gentle touch of Thy Loving Hand,
I hear softly the eternal music,
I think of listening to Thy beautiful words.
You are enough for me, for the rest of my days.

I am going back like Alexander the Great,
With hands outstretched to show that I am not taking away
any material possession.
I take with me only the good things that I did while I visited this
place.
I have to travel light and there is no checked-in baggage.
I leave them all behind eager to meet Thee, O Divine Master.

97. Unchartered waters

As I searched Google to get my answers, I did not get this one.
As I searched on facebook, I did not see that face,
As I searched for many things on Twitter, Instagram or YouTube,
I did not find this one.

I was constantly on "facebook", reluctant to face the book and read the book.
I thought I was smart when I spent all my time on smart phones,
I thought I cared for myself, when I used iPod, iPad, iPhone
I forgot about the wePods, wePads, wePhones.
My life has been quite selfish looking at my best interests –
"What's in it for me?"
You are leading me to the unchartered waters,
unknown and unfamiliar to me.

Lead me and guide me,
The road may be difficult to traverse,
When I fall, let me rise again and walk.
"Take this cup away from me... not my will, but Thine be done."

98. Deepavali

The great festival of light is celebrated, just outside my hotel.
Let me get out and join in the fun.
What a joy to my senses all these rows of lights,
What a sight to hear the crackers burst.

The tussle between the good and evil continues every day…
Every moment I am fighting to keep me on Thy way,
You are the eternal light that shines through everyone and everything,
Be my guiding light and strength all the day.

Let me not hide my lamp so that others cannot see the light
Let me spread the light of love and warmth of friendship,
As I join in these celebrations of light tonight,
Let me pledge to overcome evil with the good things that I do every day.

99. The morning dew

As soft as the morning dew, You descend into my heart, mind and soul.
As the temperature falls at night, the dew settles on the blades of grass.

Those who walk by are amazed by the dew on the green grass,
Children sometimes pick it up and place it on their eyes or cheeks to feel the dew.
I pass by the scene without having a clue,
But You know the Dew and have the Clue.

The dew reminds me of the passing nature of things…..
When the sun rises in the morning, the dew will disappear,
But when it cools at night the dew is formed again.
The dew tells me about the reality of how things appear and disappear.
Let showers of blessing descend upon me and my family, my community and my country and on everyone and everything,
Like fresh dew drops sitting pretty on the green grass.

100. Fond memories

You have created fond memories for me to remember forever,
Let me cherish these memories, l will not let them perish.
Your life has been and will be an inspiration for me,
You are not gone… You are here.

We want to celebrate your life's achievements
More than all, we want to remember the good times we have had together.
Your words of wisdom are resonating in my ears,
Your kind deeds always inspire me to go ahead.

You were loving, caring and forgiving to all who came in contact with you,
You will be missed dearly, but we will hold you dear ever in our hearts.
Your presence lighted up every gathering,
Your thoughts, words and actions inspired us all.

We will not forget the legacy you have left behind,
Your ever loving presence will always be remembered,
You are our hero, you are our leader,
We celebrate your life so that we are inspired to follow in your footsteps.

101. The crying baby

I was told and taught that only a crying baby gets milk.
So I cried and tried to get my promotion, riches and fame.
But you did not heed my cry.
Then all of a sudden, you gave me all of these.
Patience paid off just like the crying baby got fed.

I cried not knowing your reserves,
You know my innermost thoughts and desires.
You are the Divine providence, who takes care of me day by day,
I put all my trust in You.

When trials and tribulations come my way,
Let me not run away from Thee.
Let me trust in Thy love and care,
I lay all that I have at Thy feet and entrust all my talents for Thy service.

102. Every child, everywhere

Every child everywhere should be able to
Go peacefully to sleep without being hungry.
How can I sleep peacefully when these kids are hungry?
Let me be there to console and comfort the afflicted.

Children are not just hungry but are also discriminated because of their ethnicity, language, religion, culture, nationality, colour… and the list is endless.
Every child should be able to give its best shot to the best jobs available out there.
It should not be subtly or systematically denied to anyone.
Every child should be equal at the start.

In a fully conscious world, the children would be searching for happiness and fulfillment.
They would need to be fed first before they can work.
Poverty can be eradicated just like what we have done with some diseases…
We should join together to form a network to banish poverty …

Everyone has a right to live in dignity, peace and happiness,
Every child has a right to grow up in peace and prosperity.
Let our children dream and achieve their goals in peace and tranquility,
Our future as a nation and as humankind rests on these children!

103. The famine, the floods and the fires

The famine is raging in the horn of Africa and other parts of the world.
It is like a thorn in the flesh causing so much harm to the individual.
In a connected world we feel the pain
even more with all the images in the media.
We have to take the bull by the horns to solve this problem.

Every human being deserves to live a peaceful life with adequate food, clothing and shelter,
We all have to strive to achieve this goal.
It is easy to turn a blind eye of indifference, if we are not affected.
But we should empathize with the people affected by famines,
floods, fires and all other calamities…

We need to examine the root causes and
try to resolve these problems permanently.
Everyone deserves at least a minimum standard of life.
Let me contribute my share to these people so that they can live their lives in peace and contentment.
How can I be unaffected when the whole human consciousness
should arise to help those in need?

Let me make a resolve to do all I can to help those in need of
my time and money.
Let me commit any resource that I can give for their betterment.

104. Thirst for freedom

The thirst for freedom is universal.
My heart and soul cry out for this longing,
The thirst for freedom is everlasting,
My heart and soul cry out for this lasting peace.

Let no one suppress the freedom of people,
Let people live in a state where they can choose their destiny.
Let no one chain the dreams of our human race,
Let our dreams fly high, like kites in the sky.

Let no one tamper with the quest for freedom,
Freedom to live in dignity and peace.
Let no one put on bondage the genuine aspirations,
Of those who thirst for real freedom and social fairness.

Let the winds of change blow upon the face of the earth,
so that we may be transformed.
Let the bells of freedom ring loud and clear,
so that we can all live in peace and joy.

105. The language of love

The language of love is written on the face of the little child,
We need to learn that language,
Language is only a means of communication,
Proper communication would build love and trust.

All the wars and war of words in the name of languages are mere wastes,
Language is only a means of communication,
Language is a means to an end,
So let us speak politely and pleasantly to others to build communication.

We will preserve every language and the rich traditions they hold,
Every language speaks something to us and we can learn a lot from each one.
The collective wisdom from different languages enrich our human progress,
So let us learn as many as we can.

Let the language of love which goes beyond communication,
Be the strength and courage for everyone.
Let the language of love flourish,
This I will always cherish.

106. We will celebrate your life

Just as the pain of sorrow dissolves,
Let my doubts clear away,
You were the sunshine that warmed and cared for me and all of us.

We walked to the topmost mountains,
We talked of the most beautiful things.
We rhymed the best written lyrics,
Your love will always keep me going.

We went around the world searching for peace,
But now you have travelled beyond our hopping destinations,
You are gone to a permanent place of peace and joy,
We want to thank you for your love and your life.

We will celebrate your life,
You were our friend, teacher and guide.
Your vision, mission, passion and compassion will be our goals too.
Your dreams will always live through our lives forever.

107. Be my sunshine

Be my sunshine
Let me grow with you…
Ever since I met you, my life has changed,
Our friendship and love has given a new hope for my living.

Even when I get drenched in the monsoon rain,
Be my sunshine to dry me up.
Even when I slip and fall on the snow,
Be my sunshine to melt the snow away.

Even when clouds linger in the sky,
Be my sunshine behind the clouds.
Even when things go wrong in my life,
Be my sunshine and let me trust in your love and friendship.

108. Now and Wow

When I add "I" to Now, it becomes Wow.
Let me make my now a wow moment and put a spark into my life.
In my life there is a renewed zest and zeal for living.

NOW – let me live the present
The Divine has been so good to me.
Eternity is the present – I need to perform one day at a time.

Duality is there in all Thy manifestation
Matter and anti-matter, thing and nothing
But ultimately everything is just ONE.
Everything just wraps into ONE.

Our evolution is taking place at the level of consciousness, attitude and not just in the mutation of genes.
The Kingdom of God is within me.
Let me make my now a wow moment and put a spark into my life.
Let there be a renewed zest and zeal for living.

109. The Ultimate

I have been trying to grasp You beyond my imagination,
Beyond my reason, understanding and faith.
You were the light and darkness – the absence of light.
I am waiting for You with my heart gleaming,
With my hands holding my life's account.

Look with compassion on my sins and failures,
I cannot, will not and do not want to be separated from You.
For my finite failings, I ask for forgiveness,
I do not want to be infinitely separated from You.

O Divine, show Thy mercy upon me,
I know that I am towards the end of my earthly sojourn,
But with Thy help I will live the rest of my life singing Thy praises,
Let my life be lived in Thy presence.

110. The seven words of eternity

Just like the seven sounds of Music
What if there were seven words of eternity?
Is it love, joy, peace, happiness, hope, caring, sharing?
Are there any other?
You can add or modify your words to this list.

All these words point to Thee. Let me put these words to action.
They are eternal, timeless and everlasting.
These words direct us to perpetual happiness
And they show how we can emulate the Divine within us.

These words are also a call to action for all of us.
By acquiring and practicing these virtues,
We can bring tranquility and a better equality to our communities.
They show how we can stimulate the Divine presence all around us.

111. Expectation

Expectation is greater than the event,
But expectations have to be managed.
When expectations are managed right,
My whole life finds meaning and joy.

My problem is that I have been living up to the expectations of others and not according to Thy will.
I was more concerned about what others would think
rather than what You would think,
I was expecting more than what I deserved,
I was looking for great returns but very little was my reward.

Every time I set an unrealistic expectation,
For me or for others,
Every time I provide an unreachable target, unobtainable goal,
I am setting the wrong type of expectations.
Let me change my priorities and expectations to match
what You want me to do.

112. And then there was light

The light was given to us as we are still having darkness in our consciousness.
The awakening of the consciousness has to take place.
I wandered in darkness but then the light shone on me.
And then there was light.

I strayed far away from You just like a prodigal,
I wandered into the lush green pastures of pleasure.
But soon I was in the mud sitting alone and
thinking of the love that I had lost,
Love that you always had for me.

Now I rise up and stand on my feet.
I look at my past and it frightens me but when
I think of Your love it brightens me.
My past deeds blame me, but Your love and the future to be lived flames me.
Let me walk towards you… extend Your hand and hold me lest I fall again.

I know that I have shut out this beautiful light and befriended darkness,
I found it convenient to live in darkness and
the darkest nights comforted me.
Now I emerge on to the light and it dims my eyes,
But I will slowly open them to constantly enjoy the Light …
And then there was Light.

113. The dance of creation

The whole creation is dancing to an unheard tune,
Let the whole creation sit at Your feet in silence and learn from Thy wisdom.
I marvel at the change of seasons,
    the colours of life,
    the joy of birth,
    the happiness of growth,
    the hope at death.
Let Thy creation dance for joy, long for hope and love.
For Thou art in our midst.
You reveal Yourself to us in the dance of Thy creation.

The creation all around me is the biggest mystery.
My place in a known family, community, country,
in an unexplored universe is unknown in many ways.
As the experiments keep increasing,
let me marvel at the dance of creation happening all around me.

Let me join in this dance of creation,
Let me jump with joy at Thy wonderful design,
Let me hope for getting the best out of this day,
Let me dance with joy seeing the dance of creation.

114. Win peace, lose war

It is better to lose a battle or war for peace,
Than to win it and lose peace forever.
If only each of us think how we can be agents of change for peace,
If only each of us stop thinking about ourselves alone.

The process is with dialogue and not a one-sided submission or aggression,
Peace comes with the stillness of the mind,
Peace comes where the heart is not upset,
Peace comes where the fusion of this mind and heart occurs to forget and forgive.

Let my soul enter into a deep meditation to win peace even if that means losing out on some things.
I see myself as a person, who encourages conflict,
When these could be resolved through amicable dialogue.
Let me resolve to change and bat for peace,
With myself, family, community, country and the world.

115. I saw Thy face

I saw Thy face amongst the great mountains –
the Himalayas, the Rockies, the Alps, the Andes
And all other great mountain ranges.
I saw Thy face amongst the deepest valleys and the Grand Canyons…
You are there in the peaceful flow of water and you are there in the fury of the flood waters.
You are there among the dwellers of the slums and shanty towns.

I saw Thy face in the face of refugees fleeing from their dictators who were promoting genocides and for whom power is more important than their people.
I saw Thy face in the face of the downtrodden,
  the oppressed,
  the underprivileged,
Reveal Thyself to me O Divine.

I saw Thy face in the unemployed and the underemployed
I saw Thee in the faces of the helpless victims of violence,
abuse, hatred and genocide.
I saw Thee in the faces of the upright who were uprooted or falsely accused,
I saw Thee in my life and all the events that have led me so far.

Let me bring all these memories, hopes and dreams
And lay them at Thy feet.
May You change my life forever,
Reveal Thyself to me O Divine, day after day…

116. The eruption

The eruption of human greed, anger, apathy and so many other aspects
are turning our world into an inferno.
But what we need is the eruption of human consciousness,
just like a volcano
Where fairness and justice would rise like fumes from the volcano
And flow into our hearts like the molten lava.

Often the frustration that I feel is diverted into other acts
that I don't want to do.
The frustrations could come from unfair treatment, discrimination, loss of friendship etc.
Some uncaring dictators say that they care for the common good and sacrifice your personal right especially when they know the masses are powerless to question the policy makers.
Even some democracies restrict the rights and freedoms of their citizens camouflaging it with the notion of common good.
As long as their power is not in jeopardy, they continue to discriminate.
Freedom is the most expensive thing that we have as humans and any unreasonable restriction of it is against human rights.
Let us see through the ulterior motives and realize that it is done to restrict and chain its people.

The frustration faced by people can erupt into an agitation or a protest.

On a personal level these can lead to a period of depression or self-depreciation.

There is power in the collective voice of the public and let not the dictators who commit genocides ruin our lives and our freedoms.

Stand up for your rights and freedoms!

117. Empathy

If I put myself in the other person's shoes, I would attain another aspect of his current attitude.

I will be slow to judge, argue, quarrel or put down others.

Each person is a product of his genes and circumstances.

The experiences which have shaped each person have given him different meanings to each word, symbol, art, people, relationships...

With these different combinations, we can't expect people to behave exactly in the same way.

There are nuances at every stage in every person everywhere.

This is the beauty of creation that we are all different,

We are all like flowers that are part of a bouquet.

Each flower adds beauty but as a whole the bouquet looks more beautiful.

Let me be one of those flowers happy to be part of the bouquet.

The next time when people react differently to situations, I will calmly think of the permutations and combinations of situations that are at play...

Let me learn to empathize and not just to criticize...

118. One percent

The taxation in many countries is based on a progressive code.

The more you make, the more needs to be shared with the society.

But when the tax code or policies are examined it becomes clear that there are so many loopholes for some to pay less,

The middle class is really affected as they are taxed at some of the highest marginal rates.

The poor struggle to survive as the wages they earn is not sufficient.

Some people can write off many expenses and their capital gains are taxed at a much lower rate.

If we truly examine poverty, no one deserves or wants to be poor or hungry.

If we share a little bit more, the human species can differentiate itself from the animal herd in the global forests that wake up to eat or be eaten.

It's a shame that many of us make a fortune through our jobs and investments.

At the other end of the spectrum, many people are unemployed and are forced to beg for food.

If we all pull together, we can change this situation.

We can ensure that everyone has at least sufficient food to survive.

We pay so much of taxes to our countries, states, cities and municipalities for our betterment.

The taxes are really needed to run our cities with its infrastructure, hospitals, schools, police and fire departments, libraries, utilities etc…

Why don't we pay 1%, 0.1% or at least 0.01% of our after-tax-income as a “Global Tax”, so that we can wipe out abject poverty from the face of this earth?

If we want to make poverty history, we need to make it not “his story” but “our story”. Then we can truly wipe out poverty and hunger.

Let us start somewhere in this change for a better future.

Together we can share and care for each and everyone and create a better world.

My one percent can feed a hungry child, clothe an orphan, educate a downtrodden or shelter a homeless person.

No one deserves to be left behind.

When we share, prosperity will flow and behave like water levels.

The parched lands will be quenched of their thirst and wellsprings of hope, peace and love will sprout and grow…

Let me not wait any longer…it is an urgent matter.

Our one percent can root out poverty! Just give it a thought and do what you can...

119. Online, Offline

I thought of going online but the online connectivity has become an obsession and an addiction.

The good that I thought it would bring has made me a conditioned person.

I am addicted to the adventures of the online jungle and I had enough.

I have been slack in my work when I could have learnt more.

I have wasted precious seconds, minutes, hours and days...
Browsing from one news to the other, viewing videos or ads,
Logs, blogs all clog my mind.
My productivity is reduced

It is time for me to reduce my dependence on the online world.
It is time for me to go offline.
Help me, O Divine, to bring a balance to my life.
With Thy help I will balance my connectivity.

120. The wars

The Wars that scare and create scars are unnecessary events
which should not be there at all.
Innocent people suffer for no reason
and those in power acquire more power during times of war.

O Divine Master,
Why do innocent children suffer?
Why do wives lose their husbands?
    Children lose their Dads?
    For wars that are fought by Kings who may not know what they are after.
Do they really forget that they are in a war?

Just wars are justified only for a just cause where there is genocide or mass murder of the innocent and no other options are available…
Are some just wars just for war?
Who are the ones that gain by the spoils of war?
Let me meditate and remember all those who are lost to wars…
Let me pray for all the survivors who have to cope with
the after effects of war…
Let there be an evolution of the mindset…
Let us build bridges of peace and love and not walls of wars and battles…

121. Non violence

I am saddened by all the violence that takes place all over the world,
The television images show the dictators involved in genocides,
ruling the land with an iron fist.
Power and positions are more important than people and democracy.
At the altar of power and position, innocents are sacrificed as martyrs.
When will this bloodshed end?

Even after a sporting event, the hooligans take the law into their own hands.
If we are not careful, even the best in the crowd could become thugs
looting other people's property.
A moment's irrational outrage can cost emotional and economic damage.

We have to ensure that the freedom is not misused by us.
We have a responsibility to protect the lives and properties of everyone.
Violence is not justified in any situation,
As human beings we have access to other ways to
resolve our problems peacefully.

122. Nishkama Karma

Doing good deeds without expecting something in return…
This is what Nishkama Karma is all about.
These days, everywhere I look, I see selfish motives behind even good deeds.
The readiness on my part to sacrifice myself for others have declined,
I am more interested in inflating my ego, wealth and health.

In a materialistic world, many do not act unless there is a personal gain,
Many are unwilling to assimilate other's pain,
Let our attitudes change to have a "Nishkama Karma" attitude,
For that will give us contentment and peace in our lives.

This attitude is a selfless act, in which nothing is expected in return,
It is humble and simple wishing the best for others.
Though the concept is difficult to practice,
It is this attitude which can bring in contentment, peace and joy in my life.

123. Online Jungle

I am living in a connected world of the internet.

I started exploring this online jungle and soon I realized that there are things of beauty

And lots of traps which could make me fall.

The many ads, banners, windows, screens, cookies, social connections, e-mail, instant messengers…

All these lure me for my time and money.

All the time I spent on browsing needs to be controlled so that I come out acquiring the required knowledge or info and not getting addicted to it.

I had enough of this addiction.

I am determined not to keep on clicking,

Not to keep on browsing,

Not to keep on watching,

Not to keep on mailing,

Not to keep on blogging,

Not to keep on twittering.

I want to be in control once again and properly use the internet and social networks.

I will balance these activities with all other things that are important in my life.

I would prefer to go fishing than my computer being phished by some hacker,

I would prefer to eat a cookie than to be tracked by so many cookies to decipher my buying, thinking, browsing pattern.

I realize that I have been a victim of internet marketing.

I refuse to keep on clicking and end up in
the darkest corner of the internet jungle,
Where venomous serpents hide in the lush green meadows
waiting to strike and bite.
I refuse to keep on searching and end up with an empty feeling.
I refuse to keep on browsing to link the marketing ads
that popup one after the other.
My life is in my hands.
I will balance my connectivity on the internet and
properly use the modern technology.

124. Re-NEW-al

I am seeing the face of a new dawn.

The sun is rising in the east showering its golden rays on
the snow-capped mountains.

The hope is rising again,

The hope that my life is changing,

A metamorphosis has already begun.

The old characteristics are thrown away and a new person is born.

A new person renewed and with a good and strong conviction.

The old self was a time of thoughtless behaviour,

When the conscious self gave way to instant gratification and
self indulgences.

This realization is the starting point of a renewal,

Actualization of this change is sure to make me a better person.

Redemption begins NOW…

Re-NEW-al begins NOW…

125. Let it be

When things go against my wishes, let me have the courage to say - "let it be".
The understanding that Thou art guiding me gives me courage.
Thou art my Guide... lead me to greener pastures where I can ingest freely,
I can live and breathe freely in a land of freedom.

You have taken me out from my comfort zones and made me land here,
Against all odds, I have struggled to reach where I am today.
I know that you will constantly lead me in the right path,
In all humility, I say – "let it be".

When my boat of life is tossed around in waves of troubles,
When my whole life is in distress because of loss and pain,
When my entire situation is hopeless and helpless,
In all simplicity, I say – "let it be".

When those around me battle against me,
When all situations are unfavourable to me,
When everyday living becomes a migraine,
Let me live my life in peace and meekness and say – "let it be".

126. The emergence of a new self

Let my old self merge into Thy Love, O Divine,
I see the convergence of a new self and the rising of a new consciousness.
Let me love you O Master with all my heart, soul and mind,
Let every cell in my body jump with joy for
this new realization and discovery.

It has been difficult to purge my life of my habits,
It has been so easy to break my resolutions.
It has been very difficult to practice virtue,
It has been so easy to fall prey to my vices.

The old friends don't recognize this new self,
I often find myself ostracized in many ways.
The new self is filled with Thy precepts and love,
The old self longs for the ways and means of yesterday.

Let me pledge myself to live out my day in serenity and peace,
Let my days be filled with joy and laughter,
Let the new self, continue its sojourn without interruption,
Let the old self, give way to this new consciousness.

127. From the womb of continuous creativity

Our scientists translate their brilliant ideas to discover brilliant planets many light years away,
We are on our quest to find living beings in another part of the universe.
Even if we find intelligent forms of life on distant lands,
We need a logical framework to live and let live.
As creative beings, we continuously swim in the womb of eternal creativity.
Our creative works are a reflection of the all-in-one eternal creativity.

Let our creative works give rise to change,
Let our innovations produce better products and services,
Let our creativity create masterpieces of art, literature,
Let the creative works improve our lives for the better.

Innovations are taking place at a fast pace,
This interrupts the existing product, process and service champions.
Let the creative mind bring about changes to everything,
Let that change be better for humanity as a whole.

128. The final destination

I concentrate on the tombstone or the ash urn where I will be interred.

I see the two years hyphenated as my only time to perform.

The curtain opens at my birth and they close at my death.

There is no extra time granted…even if I plead with the referee.

The good goals in my life are the only goals counted in this game.

Like the Trappist monks, let me dig the grave and
bury my faults and failures,

Let me rise again as a new being, born again,
to redeem and serve my people.

I would be a better person from today onwards and
this world would be a better place.

Let me enjoy this journey as the destination can be reached anytime now.

I will stay focused on my final destination.

Though the speed and quality of travel matters,
it is the destination which is important.

Let me use all my energy to concentrate on the destination,

My thoughts, words and actions are now transformed to align
with my destination.

129. Solitude

I reflect on solitude today.
When I become aware of the stillness, I become calm and peaceful.
I move away from the busy schedules to this solitary moment.
I redeem myself in the silent moments of my life
trying to give meaning to my busy life.

I feel so much attracted to noise in my life,
Without sounds and music I cannot survive.
To settle down in silence and meditate on
Thy love and wisdom is a difficult task,
Let me love the silence that I am experiencing at this moment and love it.

In the stillness of this moment,
Let me fill my mind with positive thoughts and energy.
My short life should not be a vehicle of negativity that can travel fast and reach many destinations,
Let me enjoy this moment of solitude, this moment of endless goodness,
this moment of eternity.

130. The fall and the rise

I fall many times irrespective of my will to do good and walk straight.
It is just when I try to control my emotions that they go uncontrolled.
I do not want to fall but still I stumble upon something and fall,
Help me to rise with courage and walk again without shame and guilt.

Jesus fell three times to reach Calvary and the message is to rise again.
Many saints and venerable persons shed their lives of sin
only after many years,
These wonderful human beings show that falling is human
but rising is Divine,
Let me commit myself to rise every time I fall.

After my fall, when I don't rise it is my ego which is keeping me there.
Let me become humble enough to get up and walk acknowledging my fall.
Every failure is a challenge thrown at me to test my perseverance,
Every fall beckons me to be brave in the midst of problems and difficulties.

131. The trigger point

Let me find out the trigger points that generate anger, aggression, envy, jealousy and all other vices that I want to avoid.

Very often, it's my ego that is at play and defends myself against others.

Let me find out the trigger points that activate this.

This root cause analysis can help me to find the real problem and solve it forever giving me happiness.

The root cause may be my ego engulfed in logical thinking,
dividing everything into right and wrong.

In the quest for proving the other person's viewpoint or belief as wrong,
I spent many hours in useless quarrels without any logical conclusion.

To prove my point, I find ways and means to put down the other,

This becomes the trigger that when pulled, pulls down my whole being.

Let me avoid enabling these toxic trigger points
which can make my life very miserable,

Let me fill my mind with pleasant things acceptable in Thy sight.

Let me de-stress and take a deep and long breath,

Let me breathe in the precepts of compassion, love, selflessness.

Let me breathe out my evil inclinations and all vices,

Let the real me stand up and let the selfish ego get out.

132. Rendezvous

I am waiting for a rendezvous with my friend.

I am waiting to hold his hands, embrace him and tell him how much I had missed him.

Real friendship helps people to come together and achieve their best.

Real friends help each other to become better every day.

We have been absent from each other's lives for a long time.

I had always felt a void in my life without you.

Nostalgic feelings emanated from a longing for the good old days...

I was not my whole being without you and without your presence.

As time passes on, we too march along with our external features changing gradually.

We look different every year and time waits for no one.

But our love for each other would ever remain true and wonderful.

It is beyond the realm of time and our friendship would be part and parcel of the eternal bliss.

Let us celebrate this rendezvous and commit to our friendship and love.

133. The great human march

The great human march has begun to achieve freedom.
For too long the dictators who do ethnic cleansing and genocides have ruled us,
They crushed our freedom just because
they were in power and we were helpless.
Now we have arisen from our sleep dreaming of a better tomorrow,
Claiming a better future for everyone.

We are now fearless and want a fairer treatment,
Democracies with unfair rules fall under the same category of the dictators.
All those who suppress the minorities and the most vulnerable on ethnicity, language, religion, caste, colour or creed is over.
We are one. The humanity is one… the segregation of our society into winners and losers by allocating different rights won't be tolerated.
We need a fairer society capable of giving everyone the equal opportunity that they deserve.

People are rising up against dictators who commit genocides,
People are rising up against corruption,
People are rising up against unfair rules and treatment,
The great human march is coming along on the path of human evolution of consciousness.

134. Mind the gap

While I travelled on a London or Toronto subway, I constantly heard the announcement,

"Mind the gap".

I stopped for a moment and reflected on this constant reminder to mind the gap so that no one gets hurt.

Could there be a constant announcement to mind the gap between the rich and the poor, to build a fairer world?

Could we dream of a world with less poor, less hungry people?

The world has been plunged into a dual reality unnecessarily.

The rich are busy monitoring their account balances, asset valuations and stock positions,

The poor are busy trying to survive every day of their existence.

The concept of growing together has fallen apart,

And the whole game is amassing more wealth and power.

As I step into the tube, I again hear the voice – to mind the gap.

The hunger, poverty and misery are shames
on our common human consciousness,

They are blemishes on the modern civilization and humanity.

Don't you hear the voices of the thinking people crying for a caring world?

Let us ask what we can do and not what we cannot do or achieve…

Let us share our resources to reduce the gap and end poverty and hunger …

135. Competition to cooperation

We are living in a world of constant competition –
competition to win and achieve.
But competition is not the only reality.
We can cooperate and achieve a whole lot more,
Cooperation evokes a sense of social responsibility.
Competition purely looks at a sense of self-gratification and glorification.

In a cooperative world we can have less poor, hungry, sick people.
Food, Housing and Medicines would be more affordable for the masses.
The element of cooperation brings in more sharing and caring attitudes,
The element of competition thrives mainly on selfish interests and haughty attitudes.

Competition is needed to bring about
the best in people in many situations…
But let me commit myself to cooperation along with competition.
Cooperation does not mean the lack or end of competition,
But it means that we go beyond competition.
Let us synergise our cooperative efforts to build a better world,
a better tomorrow for everyone.

Let the corporations encourage their employees to cooperate,
Let the visions also go beyond just the present on to the big picture.
Corporations with cooperation will be a joy for the employees,
Their jobs and tasks and responsibilities would be turned into joy, tranquility and rejoicing.

136. Stay always positive

Stay always positive irrespective of the hurdles that we face in our lives,

To keep a cool head on a difficult day is difficult but it is possible, if we try.

Positivity is a form of energy that transforms us and everyone around us,

It is so contagious that it can spread like a wild fire and affect the lives of others.

What is in it if I negatively interpret everything?

What is the outcome if I think negative and treat people badly?

Let my thinking be positive and actions always be supportive,

Let my thinking be fruitful and useful to me and all others in our society.

Let Thy wisdom guide me to keep my moments positive,

Let my yearning for love and freedom begin and end with Thee.

Let the irritants and troubles be turned into pearls,

Let Thy love and mercy make me stay always positive.

137. Contentment

Contentment is the key to peace, enlightenment and salvation.
It does not compare, it does not wish bad for others,
It is content with what each one has.

Nobody's rise will upset me.
Other's growth will be an inspiration for me and not an opportunity for envy or jealousy.
I won't gang up with others to put down a person who has been promoted, won a lottery, gets better salary, is in better health, has a better car or a house…
Our natural instinct is to sideline achievers, but when we accept them there is more joy and serenity.
I ask forgiveness to Thee, O Divine, for the times
 when I sidelined others,
 oppressed the meek and the lowly to achieve my selfish goals.
I promise to be contended with all that You have given me.

The power of hate is to put down others,
The power of love is to rejoice with others.
The love of power often makes us hate others,
The love of humility does wonders in our lives.

138. Fragrant Serenade

Let me be a Fragrant Offering, acceptable in Thy sight,
I stand before Thee, O Divine, in all humility,
With a contrite and grateful heart I come to Thy presence,
I offer my life as a Fragrant Offering unto Thee.

I offer Thee all the talents that you have given me,
I return the talents with the original principal and accrued interest.
All the talents I have received is Thy gratuitous gift,
Let me offer them all as a fragrant offering and sing a fragrant serenade pleasing unto Thee.

I did not bring anything into this world and neither will I take anything of my earthly goods,
Soon I will leave this beautiful creation pleasing to my senses.
I long for peace, stillness and calm in Thy presence,
I offer these longings as a fragrant offering and
sing a fragrant serenade for Thee.

Whenever my performance graph dipped into red
I offer those moments of weakness unto Thee.
I surrender my wrongdoings and sins to be washed away in Thy love.
These shortcomings and failures, I offer them as a fragrant offering and sing a fragrant serenade pleasing unto Thee.

Aren't You the Creator and the created?

Aren't You the Brahman and the Atman?

I offer my life to Thee as a fragrant offering and
sing a fragrant serenade for Thee.

Please accept me and let me rest in Thy loving presence.

"O Divine", I thank Thee for lifting me up from the mud and
bathing me in Thy love,

Let me be a shadow of Thy love throughout my life.

I have seen Thy signs and wonders all through my life and
I thank Thee for all of them,

Accept my life as a fragrant offering acceptable in
Thy sight and let me sing this Fragrant Serenade all through my life...

Appendix

Classification by Themes

Friendship, Love	1. Friendship forever… 3. Use Objects, love people 17. L.O.W.E – Love Only Will Endure 49. Drench me in Thy Love 105. The language of love 132. Rendezvous
Freedom	73. Free to be free 104. Thirst for Freedom 133. The Great Human March
Stillness, Wellness, Silence, Enlightenment, Now	20. The Power of Silence 56. Stillness for wellness 59. Enlightenment 63. The eternal silence 69. The Zen Buddha 91. Now…Enjoy the journey 98. Deepavali 108. Now and Wow 129. Solitude

The Divine, creation, life

4. The beauty of life
16. Life is short and beautiful
21. Understanding – standing with U
27. What cannot be said in words
28. Like a shooting star
31. Play Thy Music in me
32. The spark of the Divine…
33. Gravity, Relativity, Connectivity, Creativity…
50. Divine Melody
57. God did his homework day before yesterday
66. The one dollar bill
68. The curtain has been raised
71. Time and timing
72. Eternal Intelligence
77. Work in progress
78. Serendipity
80. Light and shadow
82. Life and its functions
84. The World and the word
85. The meaning of meaning
86. Best Gift
87. The sunflower habit
90. In the Divine presence
99. The morning dew
109. The ultimate
110. The seven words of eternity
113. The dance of creation
115. I saw Thy Face

Index

CPSIA information can be obtained
at www.ICGtesting.com
Printed in the USA
FFOW01n0941261214
9804FF

9 780993 915505